A HISTORY OF COLLEGE FOOTBALL IN SOUTH CAROLINA

GLORY ON THE GRIDIRON

FRITZ P. HAMER AND JOHN DAYE

THE
History
PRESS

Published by The History Press
Charleston, SC 29403
www.historypress.net

First published 2009
Second printing 2013

Cover design by Marshall Hudson

Manufactured in the United States

ISBN 978.1.59629.627.5

Library of Congress Cataloging-in-Publication Data

Hamer, Fritz.
A history of college football in South Carolina : glory on the gridiron / Fritz Hamer
and John Daye.
p. cm.
Includes bibliographical references.
ISBN 978-1-59629-627-5
1. Football--South Carolina--History. I. Daye, John. II. Title.
GV959.52.S6H35 2009
796.33209757--dc22
2009026268

Contents

CONTENTS

List of Tables

Preface

It has always amazed us with all the interest and passion for football in the Palmetto State how little has been written about its history, save for the various books on the Carolina and Clemson rivalry and the few additional books about these teams and their special coaches. This surprising situation came into focus when the authors worked together to organize an exhibition about the history of football at the South Carolina State Museum in 2007 and 2008. The exhibition displayed a wealth of artifacts and documents that told a story that went far beyond just the Carolina-Clemson rivalry. We found out in these sources, both three and two dimensional, that smaller schools—from Furman and Wofford to The Citadel and the College of Charleston—had legacies in the game. While Furman's football legacy is long and often dominating, other colleges, even if they lacked significant winning traditions, still had players of note, some impressive games and a support system that needed to be resurrected.

Despite the ending of some programs, such as College of Charleston (1913) and Erskine College (1952), new programs took their place, albeit in a much later era. The history and traditions of such schools as Charleston Southern University, Coastal Carolina University and North Greenville University only began near the end of the last century. Nonetheless, whether a school has a long or just a short football legacy, it deserves inclusion because it was part of an athletic tradition into which every fan and player has poured energy and passion, not to mention personal funds, to turn fall Saturdays into major events for more than a century.

These traditions and passions, along with some of their stories, came out in the State Museum exhibition that opened in August 2008, and they were available for visitors to see until its close in February 2009. While we think that this museum exhibition provided new insights into football history in South Carolina, it was not meant to last. Museum exhibitions are at best temporary, whether they are up for one month or one year. They cannot provide the details and intricacies of the history they purport to examine, and museums too often lack the time and the funding to make their exhibitions permanent through published catalogues and related books. Even the growing use of virtual exhibitions through websites has only a semipermanent reality to them since even these are not designed to be permanent records.

In our mind, we thought that the subject of football history, though more than a century old, deserved a permanent record that would attempt to tie together the colleges of the state in the game over that time. As the exhibition research showed us—and as our further works since then have continued to remind us—the football history of South Carolina is detailed and complicated. We trust that this first attempt will be the start of a larger and more comprehensive study in the future.

We decided to create this book to provide a permanent record of football's history in the Palmetto State. Using college media programs, correspondence and oral histories, combined with contemporary newspaper accounts, we have tried to weave a story that is both distinctive from and similar to football's history in the rest of the country. Football had northern origins that filtered down to South Carolina. In-state rivalries soon developed, and they remain as strong today as they ever were—if not more so. But such rivalries have tended to draw only the interest of South Carolina residents, in part because until the last thirty years college teams in the state have rarely challenged college powers beyond state borders. Struggles to reach national prominence began to change in the 1980s, as will be shown, but the reasons for this national obscurity for colleges in the state is not the focus of this book; we leave that for another study. Our main purpose here is to show the local changes and development of college football from its inception to the present. What we have tried to do in this small work is give a broader overview of this history that someday can be examined in greater detail.

Acknowledgements

Many individuals and organizations have provided indispensable assistance in putting this study together. And as they did, it was always with enthusiasm and energy. Perhaps the most important assistance came from the archivists at the Special Collections of the Presbyterian College Library in Clinton. Nancy Griffith and Sarah Leckie not only located important documents about PC football history, but also graciously answered our additional research requests when we were unable to travel up to Clinton. We are extremely grateful for all of their valuable assistance on several levels. In this vein, we would also like to thank Susan G. Hiott, curator of Exhibitions of Special Collections at Clemson University, and her director, Michael Kohl; Susan Hoffius, librarian at the Waring Medical Library at MUSC in Charleston; Phillip Stone, PhD, archivist at Wofford College; Richard Haldeman of Erskine College; and Elizabeth West, university archivist at the University of South Carolina, Columbia.

In addition, we would also like to thank the following for giving permission for use of images from their institutions: Jennifer Scheetz, archivist, and her colleagues, curators Grahame Long and Jan Heister, at the Charleston Museum; Gordon C. Henry, archivist, and Matthew DeWitt, sports information director, both at Newberry College; Brian Hand, formerly sports information director at Presbyterian College; Hunter Reid, sports information director, and Dr. Gary Clark, athletic director, both of Furman University; Bill Hamilton, sports information director at South Carolina State University; and John T. Kennerly, director of McCain Library at Erskine College.

Finally, we thank Dr. Reverend William Pregnall and his wife, Joye, of Irvington, Virginia, and their nephew, Richard Pregnall, of Columbia, South Carolina, for providing details about Alex Pregnall, including a copy of a manuscript that Reverend Pregnall wrote about his father along with contemporary newspaper articles about early College of Charleston football. Lastly, we want to recognize Jane Yates, director of The Citadel Museum and Archives, for providing information and pictures concerning Citadel football. And we also want to acknowledge the encouragement and support of the staff at The History Press, especially Laura All and Ryan Finn, for making this study come to pass. There are many others whom we wish we could name who provided assistance in helping make this study possible, but space will not allow us to name them all. So to those we have left out, please know how much we appreciate your assistance.

CHAPTER 1

The Origins of Football and Its Early Decades in South Carolina

The colors of the two institutions were conspicuous. Furman's banner of purple and white floated in the air and the students wore badges of the same color...the players were dressed in canvas cloth uniforms and wore caps of purple and white. The old gold and black of Wofford was everywhere to be seen.[1]

Such was the splendor surrounding the second year of intercollegiate competition between the two upstate college rivals in January 1891 as the teams formed on the field of Wofford's home ground in Spartanburg. Although the new game of "football" had only begun to take root in the Palmetto State less than a decade before, it was gaining a significant following on these two upstate campuses. At this early stage, though, the rules were different from what they have become. In fact, it probably resembled a rugby match more than what we see in college stadiums today. Scrimmage lines were unbalanced, the forward pass was illegal and scoring a touchdown only earned four points, while the extra point, or goal as it was called then, earned two. On the sidelines there were few, if any, bleachers, but the fan support, with perhaps one hundred or more in attendance, was enthusiastic and partisan in cheering for their respective team. But as the fans of this third intercollegiate game in South Carolina cheered, it could hardly have been foreseen how the game would steadily grow from a competition between amateurs into tightly organized teams with well-paid coaches and very demanding alumni, all with a passionate desire to win.

In the early years of collegiate football, teams in the Palmetto State used faculty advisors with a personal interest in football who aided fledgling teams from the Upstate to the Lowcountry. Such people had usually played the game at a northern school before coming south. Paid coaches came later once the game was more established. Yet even though unpaid, such coaches were not supposed to coach during games. Only the team captain could give instruction during the matches. Even so, the games of this early period could become violent, and injuries followed. But this was only one of the reasons why most college presidents and their faculties discouraged football. As football took root on South Carolina campuses, professors and administrators feared that too much student attention on the game and its players distracted them from their academic pursuits. Yet these concerns had already affected colleges in the Northeast, where football began more than three decades before.

Even by the 1880s, football drew thousands of fans at some of the nation's oldest colleges. Harvard, Yale and Princeton drew students, alumni and outside support to every game during their fall seasons. And this drew the scrutiny of presidents and journalist alike as the passionate fans witnessed brutal plays in which numerous players on both sides were injured, sometimes seriously. There were even occasions when such violence led to players' deaths. By 1894, a *New York Times* writer described the Yale-Princeton contest as "two masses of humanity [coming] together with a sound like a cracking of bones of a tasty hot bird between the teeth of some hungry giant. Legs and arms and heads and feet would be apparently inextricably intermingled." After the referee blew his whistle, most of the pile would separate and become individuals again, but a few would still be lying on the field. Then on rushed the doctors with assistants to patch up a player's gashed head while another player's leg would be pulled back into place. Other injured players had sprained ankles bound and wrists bandaged. Once the injuries were mended, the referee started the game again, "another human cyclone" began and the fans roared on their respective team.[2]

While such actions alone were alarming to school officials and many journalists, there were many off-field activities that had grown just as disquieting. With growing enthusiasm for the game, the desire to win led most teams to seek top players with illegal monetary incentives and other recruiting tactics. Reports even grew that college teams brought in ringers, players who were not enrolled in the school. When the season ended, such players would suddenly disappear. This kind of activity led President Charles Eliot of Harvard to attack the college game, claiming that it was filled with "tricks, surprises and habitual violation of rules" in order to have a winning team. Such activity, on and off the field, the Harvard executive maintained, rendered students unfit for intellectual activity. While the Harvard president managed to gain a few reforms, including the outlawing of one of the most vicious newer tactics of the game, the flying wedge, his attempts to reduce violence and injury proved short-lived. Unregulated recruiting continued with cash and other incentives provided to top college recruits.[3]

When the first version of football was introduced into the United States, these concerns did not exist. The first official college match occurred in 1869 between Rutgers and Princeton. Within a few short years, it spread to many other northeastern schools, quickly establishing furious rivalries between Harvard and Yale, and Princeton and Rutgers, among many other institutions. However, during these early decades, football resembled a cross section of soccer and rugby—little on the field of play resembled today's version of American football. In the first decade of football, there were fifteen players on a side, a goal equaled one point, no one wore helmets or padding and masses of players pushed and pulled at one another to move the ball carrier forward. Although rules started to evolve with the reduction of players on a side to eleven in 1880, violent conduct, severe injuries and crazed fans soon marred games.

By the early 1890s, the journalist Edward Godkin observed with alarm that there was an "athletic craze" and that leading colleges were becoming "huge training grounds for young gladiators" where "spectators roar as roared in the Flavian amphitheatre." He charged that football had become dangerous because of the "pushing, pulling, rolling, kicking or 'slugging'" that seemed endemic. Perhaps some of the violence and injury could be attributed to meager laws of the game and lack of neutral officials. Game referees did not exist in the early decades; instead, captains of the contending sides were expected to "play fair" and "police" their teammates during play to maintain sportsmanship. Then, in 1885, the college rules committee, headed by Walter Camp of Yale, mandated an umpire at every game. Nine years later, a second official was added. In spite of introducing neutral officials at games, the growing criticism of football by journalists was nearly equaled by college presidents and their faculties. As early as 1884, a Harvard athletic committee reported that the games they witnessed had numerous instances of violence coupled with unsportsmanlike conduct.[4]

Early football's brutality was demonstrated clearest when the "flying wedge" was introduced by Harvard's eleven in 1892. The formation consisted of the biggest players forming a tight V formation, or wedge, with the smaller ball carrier running behind. Once this formation picked up speed, defenders, especially those of small stature, were literally trampled or thrust out of the way, often with serious injuries. Despite this brutality on the field, football's mass appeal continued to mount in spite of the concerns from most college presidents. Big annual rivalries between such schools as Harvard and Yale, and Princeton and Columbia, drew thousands of fans by the 1890s, with large gate receipts produced by such games. Such spectacles engendered large revenues, and consequently the need to win grew.[5]

This is what appalled Eliot and many other college presidents. Still, a few demurred and denied any problems. One of these was the future president of the United States, Woodrow Wilson. As Princeton's chief executive at the beginning of the twentieth century, he saw little need for football reforms. Although some effort at reducing injuries led to the banning of the flying wedge by 1895, problems persisted. The next crisis drew President Theodore Roosevelt into the mix at the end of the 1905 season. An enthusiastic sportsman, T.R. believed that football gave young men sound physical and mental training, but media focus on severe injuries and deaths at various levels, from prep school to college, forced his hand. College presidents and football administrators, including Walter Camp, met at the White House to coordinate meaningful reform to reduce injuries and improve sportsmanship. Recent historians have argued that the northern press exaggerated the incidents of injury and death at this time but that public outcry made it imperative that changes be made. A more formal rules committee to regulate college football, entitled the Inter-Collegiate Athletic Association, resulted from the White House meetings (the forerunner of today's National Collegiate Athletic Association or NCAA).

The new committee discouraged inducements to players to come to certain colleges and also condemned player recruiting. These attempts to clean up the game would soon be tested and ultimately fail, but a new rule would have lasting impact and change the game forever as time went on. Against Walter Camp's objections, the rules committee voted to introduce the forward pass for the year 1906. The committee hoped that this new law would open up the game, reduce devastating mass formations and thereby reduce player injuries.[6]

Back in South Carolina, where football was just starting to gain notice, neither administration at Wofford or Furman seemed as concerned about their students playing the new game as they would be a decade later. They also did not support it financially or attend the first games. The first years

This rare early action shot (circa 1910) shows a runner, possibly from the College of Charleston, going around the line of scrimmage versus an opponent, possibly Porter Military Academy, also from Charleston. Note the nose and shin guards that he and others on the field are wearing, a more common form of protection than a helmet at this time. *Courtesy of the Charleston Museum, Charleston, South Carolina.*

of college football in the Palmetto State were organized and supported by the players with at least moral support from the rest of the student bodies. As already indicated, a faculty member often helped to train players, but everything else—from uniforms and transportation to games to arranging games—was the responsibility of the players and their student managers. A faculty member served as liaison to ensure that college interests and integrity were upheld. In South Carolina, the early years of intercollegiate football were truly amateur contests little more than a step above class football competitions staged on most campuses.[7]

Baseball was the main sport on South Carolina college campuses through the 1890s, yet recreational levels of football began at some institutions by the 1880s. At what was then South Carolina College, football was already a popular sport between groups of students who seemed interested in its recreational value. In October 1888, a student wrote, in a half-joking manner, that football was good for health because after playing a game, players bloodied themselves to the point that they "never need to be bled by a physician."[8]

Wofford and Furman seemed to have gained knowledge of football prior to their first game in December 1889 through recreational contests held on their campuses. Even after the first game between the two schools, intramural contests between classes at many campuses became an annual tradition in the late fall. In 1911, after the intercollegiate season, South Carolina had a competition between the four classes for the Football Trophy. Similarly, class competitions were held on campuses from Greenville to Newberry even when intercollegiate competition was suspended at most upstate schools during the first decade of the twentieth century.[9]

Most, if not all, college football programs had the game introduced by students or faculty who had played or watched football at northern schools before coming to the Palmetto State. The most noted of these early pioneers was the future innovator and coaching legend John Heisman. An 1892 graduate of the University of Pennsylvania and a football star, in 1899 Clemson College lured him from Auburn in Alabama to lead the upstate school to its earliest football success in a brief four-year tenure. The second-highest-paid coach in South Carolina, Heisman is the most famous early college football coach in the state. Less heralded northern transplants brought the game to other state campuses, including Yale graduate Elwin Kerrison, who trained the Wofford team for the first Furman contest in 1889. It was unclear if this northern transplant had played at Yale, but he certainly must have known about the game since the Connecticut school was one of the pioneers in football with a tradition of winning championships. When South Carolina College began a varsity program in 1894, it enlisted a faculty advisor with northern roots and continued to do so until it hired its own paid coach two years later.[10]

While these northerners introduced the game, they could not coach in the modern sense of the word, at least not until Heisman took over at Clemson. Until then, only team captains could give coaching tips and direction during games. The first years of football followed this practice. No coach or trainer is mentioned in the reports for the 1891 Wofford-Furman game. Except for Clemson and South Carolina, the games between other South Carolina schools seemed genteel affairs where both sides respected the competitive spirit of the other. The Furman writer who accompanied the 1891 team to Spartanburg for the third contest described friendly and spirited cheering between the rival fans as the teams prepared for the muddy match in rain and cold wind. Although a low-scoring affair, the visitors prevailed 10–0, the opposing sides having a hotly contested game in which Wofford's tackling and blocking for its running backs was its best feature. It was mainly Furman's better teamwork

The 1898 Clemson College team picture. *Courtesy of Special Collections, Clemson University Libraries, Clemson, South Carolina.*

that seemed to overcome its host in the end. The Wofford writer concurred, although he excused the loss to insufficient practice time coupled with injuries to key players preparing for the contest.[11]

South Carolina and Clemson began varsity programs in 1894 and 1896, respectively, but none of the other state's colleges began an intercollegiate program until the new century. North of South Carolina, the University of North Carolina had begun playing a small schedule of intercollegiate games in the late 1880s, and to the west, the University of Georgia began intercollegiate playing in 1891, followed by Georgia Tech. During this first decade, South Carolina colleges occasionally scheduled these out-of-state schools.[12]

There were a few schools within the Palmetto State that began to play football that by law could not compete with South Carolina, Clemson or the small upstate schools. When South Carolina passed its new state constitution in 1895, one of the most severe clauses legalized racial segregation in all public institutions. This meant that football between black

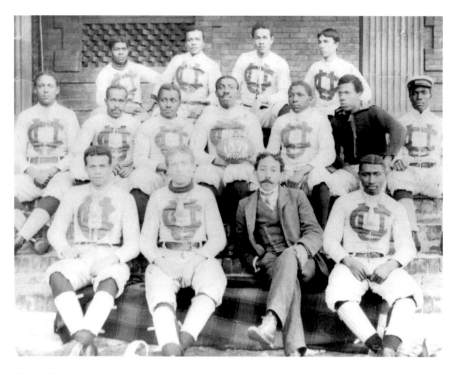

Claflin College football team, 1899. This rare early image of one of South Carolina's black college teams in Orangeburg shows that the new game of football was also becoming popular among black schools. Claflin's season record is unknown. *Courtesy of John Daye, Irmo, South Carolina.*

and white colleges was against the law. In spite of this legal impediment, football began on most black campuses early in the new century, but sadly the early records for these programs are meager, if they exist at all. In Orangeburg, privately supported Claflin College appeared to have one of the first African American college teams in the state with a squad in 1899. Unfortunately, the record for that year and several thereafter is unknown. Eight years later, Claflin's state-supported neighbor, South Carolina State College, began an intercollegiate team, defeating Morehouse College in that year's first and only contest. The following year, State College tied Allen University of Columbia and lost four other matches that season. Within three years of its first varsity season, State College became part of a segregated college league, the Georgia–South Carolina Intercollegiate Association (later renamed the South Atlantic Conference). In 1919, State College earned its first conference title. Allen University was part of this league during the same period. Little more is known about these black schools until later in the century.[13]

Eighty miles from Orangeburg, as Claflin began its first football team, Charleston colleges began playing the game on an intramural level. In 1903, the College of Charleston had its first varsity team, defeating the more experienced Furman 22–0 but losing to South Carolina 18–0. After the first year, the College did not play another team outside of Charleston for the next three years. The Lowcountry school, like some new college programs elsewhere in the state, focused its competition on locally organized teams, particularly its local YMCA, teams of former college players living in the city and even high schools. Its future town rival, The Citadel, did not begin varsity football until 1905. The small student body of barely one hundred and a very tight budget seemed to be the principal reasons for College of Charleston's focus on local competition.[14]

Just as the game was introduced to Charleston colleges, it seemed as though it would disappear from the upstate. During the 1890s, both Wofford and Furman had intermittent years when varsity football was absent. The Spartanburg school did not play intercollegiate football for a three-year period from 1897 to '99. Furman had no schedule in 1894 and then, like Wofford, had a three-year hiatus in the late 1890s. As the new century began,

College of Charleston varsity team, circa 1910. *Courtesy of the Charleston Museum, Charleston, South Carolina.*

Wofford varsity squad, circa 1900. Note that the terrier was already becoming a school mascot at this early date. In 1903, the college's trustees forbid intercollegiate competition for the next ten years, considering it a distraction from studies and appealing too much to "the primitive instincts of man." *Courtesy of the Wofford Library and Archives, Spartanburg, South Carolina.*

both schools returned to varsity play for two years, with Wofford playing its fullest schedule to date in 1901 with six games. Then intercollegiate play ended for more than a decade.[15]

As we have seen in many northeastern schools during the 1890s, there was growing concern about the violence on the field and the fan fervor over the progress and performance of their team, both of which seemingly neglected the scholarship in college. Persistent reports in the media and from some college administrators suggested that certain teams used players not enrolled in colleges for which they played. Another factor that may have had greater influence on the negative attitude of college presidents and their faculties, especially Furman and Wofford, grew out of their religious affiliations. In Alabama and Georgia, spiritual leaders of these states had begun a furious attack on football in the 1890s. Even state-supported colleges came under attack. Early in that decade, one of Auburn, Alabama's Methodist pastors listed the many broken bones and other injuries suffered in the local college's first football season. Then the pastor declared football a "foolish and useless sport" that more properly should be called "a fight." But religious writers did not just attack the action on the field, they also were quite critical of fan behavior. In 1897, the *Alabama Christian Advocate* condemned the way football games seemed "to convert a body of students, inflamed with liquor and excited by loyalty to their institution, into a howling mob of toughs, gamblers, and drunkards."[16]

Such negative sentiments from the religious fraternity were mirrored by some South Carolinians, especially at those colleges with strong religious affiliations. In 1909, Presbyterian College president William P. Jacobs editorialized in the campus newspaper that football was a brutal game that should not be allowed on a college campus, where the purpose was to train young minds. Jacobs went so far as to compare the excitement generated on the football field to "dog-fighting and chicken fighting" though they were not as injurious as football.[17]

In spite of such concerns by intellectuals and some religious leaders, the sport was popular with students on most college campuses even if they did not have an intercollegiate team to support. During the first decade of the twentieth century, college presidents of upstate colleges commented that it had become a major distraction among their student bodies. Concern that football marginalized the academic purpose of their institutions was coupled with what Wofford president Henry Snyder described as "the unadulterated spirit of battle appealing primarily to the primitive instincts of man." Furthermore, Snyder and his colleagues at Furman, Erskine and Newberry Colleges claimed that permitting football in the fall, when baseball already took up the spring term, meant that academics would be compromised year-round to the severe detriment of their small student bodies. Such concern for the academic pursuits of their institutions must have been combined with the religious affiliations.

With Furman's strong ties to the state's Southern Baptists and Wofford's close ties to the Methodist denomination, neither college could condone violent, unsportsmanlike conduct generated in many football games without attracting the ire of lay and clergy alike. Again at Presbyterian, President Jacobs considered that playing football could not be done in the spirit "of the courteous Christian." Concerns by upstate colleges that football was unchristian must have been reinforced by national press criticism of the game during this period. Columbia's *State* newspaper followed the intense criticism of football in the Northeast, especially as the season ended in December 1905. It quoted a Boston paper that claimed that football rules, as then permitted, "encouraged brutality and roughness, and put a premium on deceit." That same month, the Columbia paper reported that one of the biggest northern colleges, Columbia University, had banned football outright.[18]

Yet while Wofford and Furman dropped intercollegiate football by the 1902 season, the game at the public-supported colleges at Clemson and South Carolina continued and grew. This rivalry became more intense less than a decade after the two schools played their first contest in 1896. By 1908, one former player recalled that football was displacing baseball as the premier game on South Carolina campuses. By that time, the bitter rivalry between the two biggest schools in the Palmetto State had reached legendary proportions. The first full manifestation of the Carolina v. Clemson standoff came in the aftermath of Carolina's 1902 12–6 victory. It began shortly after the game's conclusion, when South Carolina students, with joyous fanfare, produced a "transparency" of a gamecock crowing over a crouching tiger. When they marched down Columbia's Main Street with it in their midst, Clemson students confronted them, resulting in fisticuffs, along with knives and swords for a brief period. No one was seriously hurt, but the transparency was badly damaged. Following the mêlée, the Carolina faithful returned to campus to produce another copy for use in the following day's Elks parade. Clemson cadets were livid once more. At first, efforts by authorities on both sides failed to reach a compromise. The cadets marched to the brick wall of the Horseshoe on Sumter Street, ready to storm the Carolina campus and destroy the new copy. At the last moment, cooler heads prevailed when a three-man committee from each side met and agreed to allow each side to get one half of the image and burn it before the other.[19]

While little blood was shed in 1902, in the wake of this incident Carolina's board chose to ban the Clemson game for the next seven years. Then, three years later, Carolina's board took its most drastic step: it ended intercollegiate competition for the 1906 season. The South Carolina board was convinced that the game's violent reputation had become too much for the well-being of the college's academic mission. This, combined with the frenzied interest of Carolina students and alumni about football, caused the institution's leaders to conclude that academics were being sacrificed. In truth, the students and alumni had control of athletics and the football team. During the years leading to the football ban, evidence appeared that some players for the team were not registered students, suggesting that the blacklisting of the Gamecocks by the Southern Intercollegiate Athletic Association had more truth to it than its loyal fans wanted to believe (even though the Gamecocks were not members of the organization until 1915). A special committee appointed by the board also deplored the problems with the football team. It opposed the "illegitimate use of athletics as an advertising medium for educational institutions" and was also appalled by the "abominable habit of rooting," which they urged should be discouraged. "Men who cannot win athletic contests without the aid of brass horns, bass drums and brazen lungs should be deplored." Although South Carolina leaders may have had enough evidence to support the 1906 ban, it proved short-lived. After just one season, the board voted to reinstate varsity football for the 1907 season after steady appeals from both students and alumni committees who had opposed the game's ban when it was first announced.[20]

In spite of South Carolina's drastic steps to curtail the game, the College of Charleston and The Citadel (neighbor institutions in Charleston) were starting their varsity programs and about to embark on a brief but intense rivalry of their own. Although the College began playing intercollegiate football in 1903, two years before the military college, the cadets did not take long to catch up to their city neighbors once their commandant and his board of visitors reluctantly permitted the military school to start play. But through the 1890s and the beginning of the new century, Citadel leaders fiercely opposed student petitions requesting permission to introduce football. Until late 1904, the commandant and his board believed that football would interfere with their cadets' academic and military training. With virtually every part of their day regimented with classes, military drill and chores, leaders did not see how cadets had any time for frivolous activities such as football. This concern over a full schedule, combined with reluctance to accept change, caused the military college to be one of the latecomers to the game. The catalyst that brought football to the campus seemed to grow out of a visit to the 1904 State Fair during a Clemson-Sewanee game (recall that South Carolina had suspended the Clemson game two years before). Several cadets and some board members witnessed the extraordinary play of Clemson back Rick McIver, who "put on a show." At the December board meeting, class football was permitted on campus for the first time. Surprised and delighted, the cadets formed campus teams out of their respective classes, and the following fall the first varsity team began play.[21]

During the early years, the fledgling Citadel varsity played exclusively local teams, both colleges and high schools. In this first decade of play, one of their opponents were the "Medicos," a team of medical students from the Medical College of South Carolina. During the first decade of football in the coastal city, though, one of the biggest games was the 1910 contest between the College of Charleston and The Citadel.[22]

The "Medicos." In the early years of the twentieth century, the Medical College of South Carolina in Charleston had a varsity squad that played schools in the city and beyond. This 1907 team played three games, including the Augusta medical school in Georgia. *Courtesy of Waring Medical Library, MUSC, Charleston, South Carolina.*

The Citadel on the field against an unidentified opponent in its third year of varsity competition (1907). Note the man in the dark suit facing the play; this is probably one of the two game officials. *Courtesy of Citadel Archives and Museum, Charleston, South Carolina.*

In October, The Citadel seemed poised for another win over its local rival, having a larger, more physical side compared to the smaller College squad. Furthermore, the cadets had not allowed their city rivals to score on them since 1907. Nevertheless, the bigger side was stymied all day, while the quicker, smaller "Maroons" found ways through and around the cadet defense. The culminating play of the game, sealing the upset, was devised in a huddle by Alex Pregnall, the College's speedy quarterback. Using a ruse that at the time was legal, Pregnall hid the ball under his jersey and made a dash of nearly sixty yards before the bewildered Citadel defense could tackle him a yard from the goal line. On the next play, the Charleston quarterback took it over The Citadel line for the 11–0 triumph.[23]

Such a triumph, the only one over The Citadel in the College of Charleston's brief football legacy, was followed after the game by one of the small college's biggest celebrations in the early sporting history of Charleston. In the evening, a large parade of student fans marched through several streets in the center of the city, dressed in robes of white and banging two big drums, with many mouth organs and sundry other instruments in attendance as well. Along the way, they stopped to serenade businesses and undisclosed residences, including the *Charleston News and Courier* offices.[24]

College of Charleston fan support, coupled with the near riot in Columbia eight years before, is indicative of how college football was swiftly evolving into more than a game on most campuses across the state. Winning, especially against bitter rivals, was more important than having just a sporting competition. The courteous atmosphere in the early contests between Furman and Wofford described by writers from both sides as a tough but friendly rivalry—with students and a few hundred locals "lustily" cheering on their team—had changed. As the new century began, nasty encounters between rival fans and players on the field began to resemble some of the games in the Northeast. An old alum of the South Carolina team of 1909 recalled a half-century later that in his playing days a bonfire and loud cheering began on campus the night before the Carolina-Clemson contest. If the Gamecocks were victorious, the student body had a "shirt tail parade" into downtown Columbia. At the game itself, the sidelines were jammed with overzealous fans milling about, following the progress of the ball during each play. Shouts of all kinds, including advice to their teams and game officials, were punctuated by "waving streamers, sticks and derby hats." A similar atmosphere surrounded Citadel games. Grandstands in these early years were few and often temporary, although one paid thirty-five cents to sit, while the fans who stood on the sidelines paid ten cents

Early football uniform, possibly the College of Charleston, circa 1910, from the collection of the Charleston Museum. Uniforms varied much more in these early days from today. In the first year of the Citadel football team, 1905, James H. Hammond recalled that the team had no money for uniforms, so the players were told to go through a wooden box containing old sweaters and trousers that looked like discarded baseball outfits. For equipment, Hammond made a "shoulder pad out of several laps of a heavy army blanket." *Image by Susan Dugan, Columbia, South Carolina.*

less. These supporters often stepped onto the field of play, forcing the game to be held up while officials shooed them off. Fights between rival fans made disruption of play even more prevalent.[25]

The teams on the field often showed little sportsmanship to their opponents. At Citadel games, recalled former Bulldog James Hammond, class of 1907, "Anything went and there were plenty of injuries." Smaller players carrying the ball were nearly torn apart when their linemen pushed the ball carrier forward to gain yardage while the defensive team "dragged" him by the neck to hold him back. And verbal taunts between rival players could be just as abusive. This was especially the case when a player transferred from one school to another. One former Charleston native, who had played a season at The Citadel, recalled that when he changed sides the following season to join the rival Charleston Athletics, he was cursed at regularly during the game, but in Gullah.[26]

Based on such rough, abusive behavior, it would seem, as one historian has argued, that in the early decades of college football women were excluded from the sidelines or kept segregated from boisterous male fans. Granted, few South Carolina colleges in the early twentieth century allowed female students. Those that did, and South Carolina was one, had just a small cohort of coeds, usually little more than 10 percent. Some all-male campuses, such as Furman, had a separate female campus. Young ladies who attended Furman games usually had a male escort. It seemed that unescorted women who attended came in carriages and watched the game from such a perch, somewhat protected from often rowdy male fans. In Greenville at the November 1893 Furman game, Wofford had a contingent of female fans that came from Converse, Spartanburg's college for women. Here they seemed not to be segregated from the rest of the fans. With nearly one thousand in the temporary stands, the crowd included "an array of feminine beauty that could only be produced in the genial clime of the fair South-land."[27] At other Wofford games, it seemed that female fans were more protected. The young women stood in the "neighboring piazzas," waving Wofford's black and gold covers. At the most male-oriented college in the state, The Citadel, several "female sponsors" attended the home games to encourage the team and its cadets before and during each game. Young women from the all-female Chicora College in Columbia came to Carolina games escorted by male students. After one important victory over a rival in 1910, Carolina students made a procession to Chicora to proclaim their triumph to the girls on campus.[28]

Whether the growing excitement generated by the games at Carolina, Clemson and Charleston had an impact or not, by 1913 the decade-long moratorium imposed by presidents at Furman and Wofford was wavering. Students of both schools had never liked the prohibition and each year had attempted, but failed, to have intercollegiate football reinstated. Then, at the end of 1912, Furman's student body overwhelmingly voted a three-

A Citadel cadets cheering section during a 1908 game. *Courtesy of Citadel Archives and Museum, Charleston, South Carolina.*

The first Newberry College varsity team, 1913. Although the school had played unofficial games against Edgefield in 1901, the college did not establish a formal intercollegiate squad for another decade. That first team played both high school and colleges, including trampling Bailey Military Institute in Greenwood, 159–0. *Courtesy of Newberry College Archives and Library, Newberry, South Carolina.*

man delegation from their midst to plead their case to the Furman board meeting in Abbeville in December. Although the argument used to attempt to persuade the board to suspend their ban is unrecorded, the campus had a huge celebration when their representatives telegraphed the student body back in Greenville afterward announcing the games' reinstatement. But perhaps the board had not needed too much persuasion. Seven years later, on the eve of another football season, one Furman student proclaimed that the football team had a new and significant "drawing card" with a new stadium, which would help encourage an increase in Furman's student body to five hundred. The new stadium was now more than just a way to increase school spirit; it promoted the school beyond the confines of Greenville and helped with new student recruitment.[29]

Similar arguments were changing the minds of other South Carolina colleges of the upstate. Wofford reintroduced the game a year after its Greenville rival. Newberry College officially introduced intercollegiate football for its first season in 1913. Erskine College, a Presbyterian institution in Due West, South Carolina, began its first team in 1915. Sixty miles east of Due West, its sister institution, Presbyterian College in Clinton, South Carolina, had begun play two years before. After several years of failed student petitions to the PC faculty committee, it grudgingly changed its position to permit football after reviewing a student petition with ninety signatures. Despite PC president William P. Jacobs's strong opposition to football less than a decade before, the college's leader seemed unable to resist any further. (Ironically, it was the president's son, William P. Jr., who helped introduce the game to PC, becoming its first captain and quarterback.) At each of these colleges, the student body had lobbied for several years to either reinstate the game or allow it on campus for the first time. The change of heart from so many schools just prior to the outbreak of World War I suggests that society's view on competitive college sports, especially football, was changing. With so many students and alumni eager to have a varsity team, college administrations in these upstate institutions had little choice but to rescind their bans. The possibility of losing new students appeared likely, something that none of these small colleges could afford. In the post–World War I era, such reasoning clearly replaced old opposition to intercollegiate football.[30]

CHAPTER 2

College Football

Growing into a Campus Tradition

O nce the armistice was signed in November 1918 ending the Great War, the reduced football schedules on South Carolina's college campuses were ready to surge ahead with longer seasons and improved facilities. The only exception was the diminutive College of Charleston, with its student body of barely one hundred and a miniscule budget: 1913 was its last season on the gridiron. During the College's last two seasons, its teams earned just one victory in ten games, ending its last season with embarrassing defeats to its Citadel rivals 72–0, and Newberry 39–0.[31]

In spite of the demise of football at the College of Charleston, the rest of the state's schools continued with improved student and financial support. While a few colleges had become members of athletic conferences prior to World War I, those that had stayed as independents began to reconsider their status. By the postwar years, the Southern Intercollegiate Athletic Association, begun in 1895, had grown to include several more South Carolina colleges along with many schools in Georgia, North Carolina and Alabama. In 1921, several schools, including Clemson, split away to form the Southern Conference. The new conference wanted to forbid freshmen from playing on the varsity and prohibit its college players from playing summer baseball for money. Such an association with formal rules attempted to regulate team behavior on and off the field with regard to recruiting and conference championships. Within the state college ranks, the prestige of winning the most games became a semiofficial state title at the end of each season.[32]

In 1919, Furman began a run of state titles that surpassed all the other state colleges through the twenties. Any qualms from the Furman administration about football had disappeared. For the 1919 season, the new ten-thousand-seat Manly Stadium was inaugurated. This facility, combined with better players and a young, successful coach, Billy Laval, witnessed the Baptist-affiliated school dominate the Palmetto college ranks with six state titles through 1927. By the 1922 season, Furman professor W.H. Coleman proudly wrote that students and faculty were united in their support of the football team in its mounting success: "The strong, clean teams that have represented Furman on diamond and gridiron…have added new brilliance to the name and fame of Furman." The Greenville college's strong football team gave the institution bigger name recognition, which many students and faculty thought attracted not only better athletes but more new students in general.[33]

Early in Furman's mastery of the state's intercollegiate competition, the university received its original nickname that would stick with it until the 1960s. During a dominating game against Newberry in 1920, fans on the sidelines began referring to Furman's offense as behaving like a "hurricane" against the outmanned Newberry squad. Shortly after that, Furman fans and alumni began referring to their team as the "Purple Hurricane," purple being the school colors. This remained the football team's name until 1963, when a student poll was taken to vote on renaming all of its varsity teams. Following that vote, the "Paladins" name won and has remained Furman's nickname for more than four decades.[34]

None of the other state schools could claim such a record, but all tried to build winning programs through hiring better coaches and recruiting top players. Clemson and Carolina built on their rivalry that had been cemented before 1917. Clemson succeeded in challenging Furman in the late twenties. After the 1927 season, Carolina went to the extreme of luring Furman's successful coach, Billy Laval, to Columbia. Although after his second season the new coach admonished Carolina's student body for lacking sufficient spirit and commitment to the football team, there still were some spirited fans for the Gamecocks. This spirit was embodied best by the "Cheerios," the official student cheering section, numbering 275. Even with a loss to Clemson in 1929, the annual rivalry between the two state schools drew 14,000 fans. Despite indifferent records on the field, interest in the Gamecocks never waned.[35]

Clemson and South Carolina had 5-5 records against each other during the decade, and although they had some notable wins during the decade,

Wofford versus Presbyterian College, circa 1919. Note that at least some players are not wearing helmets. Into the 1920s, some players still refused to wear such protection, considering such equipment unmanly. Helmets did not become mandatory in NCAA rules until 1939. *Courtesy of Wofford College Archives, Spartanburg, South Carolina.*

A University of South Carolina leather pennant, with painted letters and school emblem. This rare artifact belonged to freshman George Meeks, who used it during the 1922 football season. The family is not sure if George bought it then or acquired it before he went to Carolina. He left school at the end of his first year and never returned. *From the collection of George Meeks, nephew. Image by Susan Dugan, Columbia, South Carolina.*

they never had consistent success against Furman. Heading into the 1929 Clemson showdown, South Carolina was 5-0 and really appeared to be headed for glory. But suddenly, the surging optimism of the first five games evaporated on Big Thursday. The underdog Tigers "put a tragic ending [to] Billy Laval's sensational victory parade," crushing the Gamecocks 32–0. The Columbia school finished the season with two ties, one victory and one loss, seemingly unable to fully recover from the stunning defeat to its arch rival. As for the Tigers, they had some more success later in the season, but it was somewhat diminished by three defeats, including one to Ole Miss a week after their big win over South Carolina. While both schools finished 8-3 that year, they did not have winning consistency during the 1930s. After 1930, the Tigers had three straight losing seasons before beginning a steady but slow improvement up to 1938, when the Tigers went 7-1-1. Then the following year, Clemson almost went undefeated, losing just once, by a point, to Tulane in the first game of the season. Following the season, the upstate college accepted its first bowl invitation to the Cotton Bowl, winning a close one against Boston College, 6–3.[36]

From 1919 until 1928 Clemson won just one contest against the Purple Hurricane of Furman. The Greenville school had six wins and two ties over that span against the Tigers. Similarly, other schools in the Palmetto State, from Erskine to Wofford to The Citadel in Charleston, had modest football records. After Erskine had some of its best years in 1920 and '21—including its only win over Clemson in 1921—the Due West squad, known then as the Seceders, had several dismal seasons with rarely more than one victory in each year until 1929. Nonetheless, the students and administration continued to support the team, both financially and emotionally. Likewise, Wofford had few wins to boast about during the decade, losing all six games against Furman.

Even after the 1929 stock market crash and the ensuing Depression of the 1930s, reduced budgets suffered by all colleges in the Palmetto State did not dampen interest in football among students and alumni. By 1934, South Carolina began playing its home games in the new Municipal Stadium at the state fairgrounds in Columbia. The concrete stands replaced the old wooden ones, with an improved fan capacity of fourteen thousand. This is the origin of today's Williams-Brice Stadium that now has a capacity of more than eighty thousand! Likewise, during the same decade, Furman moved out of Manly Stadium into Sirrine Stadium in 1936, with a seating capacity of more than eighteen thousand.

Above: Newberry College playing an unidentified opponent, 1928. *Courtesy of Newberry College Archives, Newberry, South Carolina.*

Left: Charles Cain, Gamecock player, circa 1930. The bull's-eye design on his jersey was first popularized by Furman coach Billy Laval during the early 1920s. Although player numbers on uniforms were recommended in 1915, the NCAA did not require them on the front until the late 1930s. *Courtesy of the South Carolina State Museum, Columbia, South Carolina.*

Such growth in new stadia in the midst of economic depression was aided by New Deal money provided from the federal government, which was desperate to find work for thousands of unemployed workers. However, at the same time, the construction of such facilities showed that college football was firmly a part of the campus scene throughout the state, as it was in the nation. By the 1920s, the coaches' salaries at the state's two biggest colleges were becoming the highest in the Palmetto State. In 1920, South Carolina, in order to improve on its mediocre record, hired Sol Metzger, a nationally recognized coach who had created several top teams at the University of Pennsylvania, for $6,000.00 ($61,616.19 in 2007 dollars). His salary was $1,000 higher than university president William D. Melton's own. In the upstate, Clemson's football coach earned a similar salary rivaling that of his school president.[37]

On the other hand, smaller schools in the state rarely had the budget to hire big-time coaches of the day. But at Presbyterian College, they found perhaps one of the state's most dedicated football coaches of the first half-century in South Carolina. Walter Johnson, a Wisconsin native, was hired by the Clinton institution in 1915 to take over a fledgling football team, as well as build up the rest of the college's intercollegiate athletics. An athlete of note in his hometown of Milwaukee, he played football at Battle Creek College and then entered coaching after graduation while studying at three schools for postgraduate work, including Northwestern University. When he began his tenure at PC in the fall of 1915, fourteen students came to try out at his first team practice. Nonetheless, with this small number, he molded together a winning team that season that earned victories in five of seven contests.

The following two seasons, Johnson continued to put the small school on the map. Along with directing the football team, he also coached baseball and basketball in the winter and spring. After the 1917 season, he left for national service, becoming YMCA director for Camp Sevier in Greenville, South Carolina, and later transferring to Camp Custer in Michigan before going overseas for fourteen months. Upon his return in the summer of 1919, he resumed his coaching duties for the fall season. There he would continue to develop competitive football teams that had some of the best ethical standards in the state. Through his dedicated efforts, he developed the college's athletic programs beyond the big three, including track, tennis and swimming, while also directing the fundraising to build a swimming pool, a fine football stadium and a track. After twenty years leading PC's athletic teams, the school newspaper praised the Wisconsin native for making men

Walter Johnson, circa 1925, Presbyterian College's coach and athletic director who symbolized the ideals of sportsmanship and dedication to the school from his arrival on campus in 1915 until his death in 1958. *Courtesy of Presbyterian College Special Collections, Clinton, South Carolina.*

of his players, whom he always "placed…above the team." PC students and administrators recognized Coach Johnson for his teams' "Fair Play, hard work [and] clean sportsmanship"— even his competitors took notice. For the 1940 Clemson game, the upstate college recognized his dedication to fair play for more than two decades by switching its scheduled home game to Clinton, where Clemson students presented him with an engraved desk set.

Although Johnson coached his last football season that year, returning to serve his country again in World War II, he came back to Clinton in 1946 as athletics director and professor of physical education, where he remained until his death in 1958. While Johnson often had fewer resources than most colleges in the state, he produced fourteen winning seasons. PC's best years came in 1917 (8-1) and 1930 (9-1). Even though the Clinton college's eleven had several losing seasons after 1930, in Johnson's last three years as head coach he still managed three winning seasons. In spite of the rough years that periodically occurred in his two and a half decades, PC administrations and students never seemed to waver in their support of Johnson. Perhaps because of the tough schedule he always had, taking on the likes of Clemson and South Carolina throughout the 1920s and '30s, his fans admired his efforts to play these bigger schools while having regular wins over the evolving rivalry twenty miles south with Newberry College; beating other schools of that size consistently provided enough pleasure to satisfy students and alumni alike.

While small college coaches such as Johnson won respect from their larger college competitors, there was another small group of colleges in the state that played the game with as much desire and passion that were barely noticed, if at all, outside their own small fraternity. These were the black colleges that had more campus spirit than financial support during the age of Jim Crow. Until the civil rights era began to take effect in the

Allen University football squad in 1927. Allen played intercollegiate football until 1966, with big rivalries against Benedict College, located across the street, and South Carolina State College. *Courtesy of the South Carolina State Museum, Columbia, South Carolina.*

late 1960s, ending segregation laws in the South, separate black college leagues operated almost unnoticed in the mainstream media. While South Carolina State College, Benedict College and Allen University might have been ignored by white journalists, these institutions developed great rivalries that lasted into the 1960s. Then, as integration began to take effect in white colleges, the segregated high schools that had supplied the players to black institutions saw their top athletes spurn the institutions of their fathers and accept athletic scholarships to wealthier, white colleges by the early 1970s. Until then, black talent on southern football fields was almost exclusively confined to segregated leagues. Sadly, the exploits of the teams and players of these black colleges are poorly preserved in the records. Evidence available to scholars today indicates that South Carolina State had annual games against its sister schools in Columbia, about thirty-seven miles northeast of Orangeburg. South Carolina State played other teams outside the state including Tuskegee Institute in Alabama, Florida A&M and North Carolina A&T, to name just a few. After winning its first conference title in 1919 in the Georgia-Carolina Athletic Association, the Bulldogs earned a second

South Carolina State College varsity squad, 1925, after nearly two decades of intercollegiate competition against other black colleges inside and outside the state. *Courtesy of South Carolina State Athletic Department, Orangeburg, South Carolina.*

Benedict College fans at a home game in Columbia, circa 1930. Note the formalwear of most in the stands. *Courtesy of South Carolina State Museum, Columbia, South Carolina.*

conference title in 1928 in the renamed South Atlantic Conference with a perfect 7-0 conference record.

In 1935, South Carolina State joined the Southern Intercollegiate Athletic Conference (SIAC), in which Benedict and Claflin already played. The dedicated, legendary coach Oliver Dawson began coaching football in 1937 and later headed up State College's basketball, tennis and golf teams until the 1950s. During that time, Dawson achieved another hallmark in the football legacy of the school by having an undefeated regular season in 1947, from which they earned the right to play Shaw University (Raleigh, North Carolina) for the black college football title in Washington, D.C., losing 8–0.

POSTWAR FINANCING FOR COLLEGE FOOTBALL

As college football rivalries became annual traditions on campuses from Clemson and Greenville to Columbia and Charleston, the financial commitment made to college football grew steadily. This was manifested first in the hiring of coaches and their assistants. As already indicated, Carolina and Clemson paid their first coaches after just a few years of starting varsity football. Data for coaching salaries and contracts are fragmentary, but some sense of the importance of their jobs in college life became clear for many schools. Within two years of starting its football program in 1913, Presbyterian College hired Walter Johnson to coach not only football but also baseball and basketball. Soon he began other varsity programs, including tennis, golf and boxing. Although his first contract when he arrived at PC in 1915 is unknown, by 1924 he was paid an annual salary of $3,000.00 ($36,095.93 in 2007 dollars).[38] One of the top wage earners of any faculty or administrator on the campus, Johnson really earned it. Not only did he have to coach and administrate several different teams each academic year, but he also had to raise funds to develop the facilities that included a stadium, gymnasium and track at the same time. To assist him in coaching, he had only one full-time person. By 1928, this was Lonnie McMillian, a former star of earlier PC teams, who received $2,650.00 ($31,509.02). By then, his boss had a salary of $5,000.00 ($60,017.18).[39]

As PC began to feel the full impact of the Great Depression by the mid-1930s, both coaches took pay cuts, just like other staff and faculty on campus. Between 1934 and 1938, Johnson's salary was reduced by $1,000 annually. North of Clinton, in the northwestern portion of the state, as Johnson began his last season as the PC football coach (1940), a new head coach at Clemson was named to replace Jess Neely: his assistant, Frank Howard, was hired at the salary of $5,000.00 ($73,185.44 in 2007 dollars). Howard began his career as an assistant in 1933 with the Tigers but also had responsibilities in the off-season directing the baseball and track teams. By the end of World War II, Howard could focus his full attention on football, although he was named the athletics director as well.[40]

As football grew into a fall tradition on South Carolina colleges in the 1920s and '30s, it became more expensive each year to field a competitive team that had good prospects of winning. Although students on campus began to contribute toward the football budget with student activity fees before World War I, most college teams relied heavily on the gate receipts of home games to finance coaches' salaries, scholarships, field maintenance and travel. At Presbyterian College, Coach Johnson put together his football budget for the 1935 season. In it, he expected to make $6,175.00 ($92,393.21 in 2007 dollars) from gate receipts from nine home and away games along with five freshman contests. With his two biggest expenses in equipment ($1,500.00) and travel for away games ($1,450.00), he still expected that at the football season's conclusion he would clear $1,835.00 after all other expenses were paid.[41]

Although alumni of each college made contributions, a formal mechanism to raise athletic funds annually did not appear until the early thirties. One of the most well-known fundraising groups in South Carolina college football is IPTAY, Clemson's fundraising organization for its athletic program. According to one story, it was initiated following a huge upset loss to Wofford in 1933. Following the defeat, Head Coach Jess Neely stated that to improve the Tigers he needed $10,000 beyond his standard recruiting budget. Two men, one a university professor and the other a businessman, took on the job of soliciting funds during the summer, going from one alumnus to another, "more or less beating people over the head for a $10 contribution." And that is how the group began, the name initially standing for "I Pay Ten [Dollars] A Year."[42]

With time it became more sophisticated and organized, growing a large staff with local IPTAY directors for each county in the state and others for neighboring states. By this method, Clemson athletics has improved its position in recruiting and steadily upgraded its athletic facilities over time. Whether the first IPTAY drive that raised $10,000 had significant impact on the football team's improving record after its formation in the following years is difficult to say, but from 1934 on, the Tigers' record steadily improved.

After their disastrous loss to Wofford and a dismal season in which Clemson ended 3-6-2, there was a steady improvement: going 5-4 the next year until 1940, when they went 6-2-1 and won the Southern Conference and an invitation to their first bowl game.[43]

No other college in the state evolved such a fundraising organization for its athletics program, but every school had booster clubs that organized to help their athletic teams but particularly their football squads, the most expensive sport of any institution. One of the first small schools in the state to organize a fundraising arm somewhat on the lines of Clemson's IPTAY was Presbyterian College and its Walter Johnson Club. Started in 1937 by the Alumni Athletic Committee, it had a modest beginning and had only raised a total of $4,431 between 1939 and 1946 (sadly, records from the first three years of the club were destroyed when the athletic offices were turned over to an air force training detachment in World War II). After the war, the WJ Club was reorganized, and with the help of several dedicated alumni it had grown substantially by the 1960s. In the '60s, the club became one arm of a larger fundraising campaign with the establishment of the Annual Alumni Giving Fund of "Living Endowment." Although the effects of this athletic fundraising arm were considerably more modest than that of Clemson, some tangible impact of the improved fundraising at PC may have helped, in part, in the Blue Hose earning a berth in the 1960 Tangerine Bowl.[44]

By the beginning of the Depression, every college had an alumni association that made one of its goals each year to raise funds for the athletics program. Students at each institution began to contribute a portion of their activity fees toward their college team, yet none could compete with IPTAY for raising regular funds each year until the 1970s and '80s. In 1939, after South Carolina athletics ran up a debt of $120,000 and failed to make tuition payments for some student athletes, the university had to make up the difference. The original Gamecock Club, known then as the BAM (Buck-A-Month) Club, began in the late '30s to raise private funds for cash-strapped athletics at the Columbia institution. It was revamped in 1942 and placed under the control of the new athletic committee organized by the university board to administer the school's athletic program. But the new committee came under the control of board chair Sol Blatt. The 1917 Carolina graduate ran it with little or no oversight from the main university board. The Gamecock Club has continued to flourish and remains, like IPTAY at Clemson, the main source of private resources for South Carolina athletics.[45]

In spite of the economic hits that colleges across the nation had to endure in the Depression of the 1930s, South Carolina schools continued to develop their football programs. By the late '30s, Clemson began to receive its first national recognition. The first player in the state to receive All-American honors was the versatile, speedy running back Banks McFadden. At the end of the 1939 season, the Tigers were selected for their first post-season game, the Cotton Bowl in Dallas, Texas, to take on Boston College. The hard-fought defensive struggle ended in a 6–3 victory for Clemson.[46]

Clemson's rival in the Midlands of South Carolina had its first All-American three years later when Lou Sossamon of Gaffney, South Carolina, earned second team honors as a hard-hitting center for the Gamecocks. Despite the team's disappointing 1942 season, Sossamon's three years of athletic achievements on the football field overcame the negatives of a losing season. Carolina would earn its first bowl invitation in 1945 when it took on Wake Forest. Although the Columbia school lost its first post-season game, 26–14, Carolina was somewhat fortunate for even being selected since it had only a modest two victories, three losses and three ties that season.[47]

CHAPTER 3

College Football after 1945

The Modern Era

In spite of the modest records of Carolina from the 1930s and 1940s, the school began to emerge as one of the two state colleges that would deemphasize its competition with other state schools. With Clemson, the Columbia campus scheduled more games against large college programs beyond the borders of the state, especially doing so after the arrival of Rex Enright. Both schools continued to compete as members of the Southern Conference until 1953. Carolina played three smaller state schools each season from 1946 to 1952, but the rest of its schedule included larger colleges in North Carolina and Georgia and occasionally others farther afield, such as Army and Miami. Likewise, Clemson scheduled larger schools from 1946 forward but usually just two in-state opponents along with the annual Big Thursday game. For Carolina at this time, Furman and The Citadel were usually their in-state games, while for Clemson, Presbyterian and Furman appeared annually.

Then the smaller South Carolina schools with lesser budgets found that they rarely could compete on the same field as equals as in the prewar period. It was during this early postwar era that Presbyterian coach Lonnie McMillian—whose team seemed to become the season opener, and "punching bag," for the Clemson Tigers from 1946 through 1952—coined the nickname for Clemson Memorial Stadium. The PC coach started calling the Tigers' home field "Death Valley," a nickname that Clemson fans still fondly claim. PC was dominated every year by 35 or more points, losing the 1949 game 69–0, one of four losses by 50 or more points. While Furman seemed better able to compete against the Tigers than the Clinton college, there was only one game in which the Hurricane kept the final score to a single touchdown in the 1949 season.[48]

Along with bigger budgets, Carolina and Clemson began to bring in more recruits from outside the state, even looking outside the confines of the Southeast more than they had prior to World War II. Although most state colleges had brought in recruits from outside the region before, such as Dom Fusci of Greenwich Village, New York, in 1942, as well as tight end Jim Crouch of Washington, D.C., in the 1920 team, more players were recruited who had ties to other states beyond the Carolinas and Georgia. For the 1948 squad, Carolina had nine players who came from states outside of the Southeast on a total roster numbered at fifty-eight. Seven years later, for the 1955 season, the Gamecocks had fourteen players from above the Mason-Dixon line on a total roster of sixty players. Although South Carolina natives were still the majority, it appeared that Enright, Carolina's head coach during this period, wanted to find new talent from the North to improve his chance for victories.[49]

In 1959, Clemson had fifteen northern players on its roster of fifty-five. Like Carolina, its roster consisted of a majority of South Carolina natives, several more from Georgia and a few from Alabama and Florida. Although Frank Howard, Clemson's colorful head coach, was an Alabama native, he had assistants and contacts inside and outside the Palmetto State who helped him find recruits.[50]

Although the smaller colleges of the state had their sprinkling of non–South Carolina players, in the decade after World War II and into the 1960s, institutions such as Furman and Presbyterian had smaller rosters and less scholarship money and thus fewer opportunities to attract recruits from outside South Carolina and its neighboring states.

Unlike today, player recruiting was not based on detailed player studies and recruiting services. Head coaches and their assistants kept in touch with high school coaches and also relied on alumni to find talent. Eugene Moore, a Lake City, South Carolina high school star, recalled that Clemson and Carolina recruited him during his senior year in 1945. A strong lineman, Moore met Howard in Lake City, as did Enright. Although the Lake City star did visit Columbia, he found the atmosphere in rural Clemson better given his roots on his parents' farm. With that, it was not hard for him to choose Clemson. Dom Fusci had grown up in the borough of Brooklyn in New York City. Recruited by several schools, including the Naval Academy, Fusci first learned about South Carolina when Coach Enright met him in a hotel lobby while on a visit to the city. He invited the Greenwich Village native to come south and try out. Fusci took a train to Columbia to work out with some assistant coaches in the spring of 1942. After they put him through some drills and clocked his speed, South Carolina offered him a scholarship that he accepted.[51]

Like today's college recruits, high school stars in the postwar era did not necessarily prove as good once they reached the college ranks. However, one of Enright's best decisions during his tenure at Carolina was taking a tip about a little-known prospect out of Chicago, Illinois: Steve Wadiak. Enright, who had grown up in Illinois, had enough people in the Midwest on whom he could rely for prospects. Since few colleges were competing for the Chicago prospect's services, Enright's offer to the older player was quickly accepted once it was made. In 1948, Wadiak headed to Columbia to eventually become one of the Gamecocks' most celebrated running backs in the college's history.[52]

Clemson had its own success with tips from various sources. Frank Gillespie of West Virginia became one of the Tigers' top players in the late '40s. Knowing little about him, Howard invited the prospective lineman for a tryout. In those days, Clemson's young coach was nimble enough that he took on some prospects by putting on the pads himself. Howard told the West Virginia visitor to hit him. Gillespie did it with such power that Clemson's head coach ended the tryout immediately and awarded him a scholarship soon after. Not only did Gillespie prove to be one of the Tigers' top linemen, but he also played on the varsity basketball and baseball squads while double majoring in electrical engineering and textile engineering (1946–48).[53]

CHANGES AND NEW ATHLETIC CONFERENCES AFTER 1945

Both South Carolina and Clemson had been members of the Southern Conference along with most of the other colleges in the state and close to thirty other institutions in the Southeast. But after World War II, football began another resurgence. Several college programs that had been suspended for the duration, specifically Furman, Wofford and Erskine, restarted their programs. Both of the state's largest colleges began to grow both their student bodies and their football rosters at a greater rate than the other schools in the state. By 1952, the bigger schools in North Carolina, Maryland, Virginia and South Carolina came together to form a new conference called the Atlantic Coast Conference. This new conference has become noted mostly for its basketball rivalries, but football was originally the main reason for

A Clemson running back in action, circa 1955, opponent unknown. *Courtesy of Special Collections, Clemson University Libraries, Clemson, South Carolina.*

establishing a new conference with geographically related schools. The first season for football was 1953, in which Maryland won the first conference title. Clemson won its first ACC title in 1956, representing the conference in the Orange Bowl against the University of Colorado. Since then the Tigers have won a total of twelve conference titles. South Carolina earned a conference championship only once, during the 1969 season, before it opted to leave the ACC and become an independent in 1971.[54]

Although the ACC has become one of the premier athletic conferences in the nation, it was not the first major conference in the region. At its height, the Southern Conference had boasted more than forty schools throughout the Southeast. All South Carolina colleges were members during the 1920s, but by 1932 schools outside of South Carolina decided to form the Southeastern Conference. Its charter members included Alabama, Auburn, Georgia and Louisiana State. Other schools in this conference in its early years included Sewanee (the University of the South in Tennessee), University of Tennessee and Georgia Tech. While Sewanee left the conference by the 1940s, Georgia Tech would stay until 1964. In the 1990s, conferences added new teams that they thought could improve their competition and add further TV revenue; both the ACC and the SEC added new teams. The geographic boundaries that had limited who could be a member when these conferences were originally established had changed. In part because of faster air travel options that allowed teams to reach host schools, along with the desire to increase revenue, the ACC admitted colleges that would never have received consideration a generation before. The University of Miami, Virginia Tech and even Boston College became ACC members in 2003. More than a decade before, Florida State had been admitted into the ACC. The SEC, which had courted Miami and Florida State without success during the late 1980s and early '90s, accepted Arkansas and the University of South Carolina as new SEC schools for the 1993 season. Arkansas, an original member of the Southwest Conference, left as this once nationally recognized organization dissolved, with most of its members joining the Big Eight Conference, making it the Big Twelve. South Carolina, having had some success as an independent after it had left the ACC in 1971, had found it more difficult in the 1980s for its football team to gain enough top opposition and sufficient TV revenue. The chance to join the SEC gave the school just the type of competition it needed to improve its national standing and thus better TV exposure. On the other hand, as of 2008, it still has never earned a conference title, and only one basketball SEC title, since joining.[55]

The state's smaller colleges have competed in lower divisions of the NCAA or in the NAIA since the ACC took the two biggest institutions into its fold. Organized in 1921, the Southern Conference had taken the place of the Southeast's oldest athletic conference, the Southern Intercollegiate Athletic Conference, which had begun operation in 1896. Furman and The Citadel are two of the longest-serving members at this time (2009), both joining the Southern Conference in 1936. Until late in the twentieth century, they were the only South Carolina colleges that were members that competed at the Division I-AA level. Wofford, which had competed in the NAIA in the 1960s and 1970s before joining the NCAA Division II level in the 1980s and early 1990s, chose to increase its level of play, joining the Southern Conference in 1997. In 2005, Presbyterian College applied for membership in the Big South Conference and by the 2011 season will be able to compete for the football conference championship.[56]

Until its new status, Presbyterian College had been a Division II NCAA school whose in-state competition included Newberry. During the Johnson coaching tenure (1915–40), PC was a member of the "Little Four" in South Carolina (the other three were Erskine, Newberry and Wofford).

A South Carolina student standing before a mock-up of a Clemson Tiger, hours before the annual Tiger burn held at the Horseshoe on USC campus, 1945. *Courtesy of the South Carolina State Museum, Columbia, South Carolina.*

Although until the postwar era competition levels were indistinct—and, as shown earlier, smaller schools often competed on even terms against bigger schools—PC rarely defeated the likes of Clemson and South Carolina. They still kept the score close and, occasionally, defeated the bigger schools. Before 1932, PC actually defeated the Tigers twice, 14–9 in 1925 and 14–0 the following year, and both games were played on Clemson's home field. After these rare victories, PC achieved only one tie, 6–6, in 1933, losing all the remainder in that decade to the Tigers, some by large scores, such as the 1937 contest, 47–0. PC did a little better against South Carolina during this period, achieving four victories against the Gamecocks. But against other South Carolina schools it had winning records, dominating Wofford, Newberry and Erskine while winning just under half of its games with Furman and Citadel.[57]

Left: Danny Brabham, Newberry College star quarterback, grimacing during a game against arch rivals Presbyterian College, 1955. Despite his broken hand suffered before the game, Brabham led Newberry to victory that year to win the Bronze Derby. *Courtesy of Danny Brabham, Columbia, South Carolina.*

Below: Newberry College varsity, circa 1988. *Courtesy of Newberry College Archives, Newberry, South Carolina.*

In the postwar period, when the NAIA was formed, Newberry and PC saw their longstanding annual rivalry take on a more intense meaning beginning in the 1948 season with the establishment of the Bronze Derby game played each Thanksgiving. Although the two schools had played each other nearly every year since the two began football before World War I, the Bronze Derby contest grew out of an incident during a Newberry-PC basketball contest in January 1948. After the 1956 season, the rivalry focused on the annual Thanksgiving football game until PC announced its plans to move up to the Division I-AA level, playing the last Derby game in 2006. That final contest ended with PC winning 10–0, taking home the trophy for the thirty-sixth and last time since the first Derby game (Newberry was victorious twenty-one times and there were three ties in that period).[58]

Although Newberry and Presbyterian had a long, contested rivalry that lasted nearly a century, the only notable national recognition either school achieved on the football field came to Clinton in 1959 when it earned a berth in the January 1960 Tangerine Bowl. During the season, PC went to Furman's home field, eking out a 24–23 victory, one of only four achieved over the then Purple Hurricane. After this first game of the season, the Blue Hose racked up seven more wins and went to Orlando, Florida, for its rare post-season game, taking on Middle Tennessee State and losing a tight contest, 21–12.[59]

As these changes occurred within the white college football scene after 1945, black colleges in the state continued their competition and changed as well. Allen University had joined the Southern Intercollegiate Athletic Conference (SIAC). While the smallest of the three main black colleges in the state, Allen produced competitive teams to occasionally defeat its bigger rivals, although in one of its last seasons before ending football in the late '60s it went 3-6. It was during the post–World War II era that Benedict had some of its best teams, earning winning seasons through the second half of the 1940s and continuing its success into the next decade. In 1959, the Pumpkin Classic began as an annual contest against its biggest rival, South Carolina State. The following year, the Thanksgiving Day classic ended in a thrilling 48–30 Benedict victory, concluding with a superb 7-2 record. Although the Columbia institution had more winning seasons, culminating in a conference championship in 1965, its progress ended abruptly after the 1966 season because of large cost overruns that the cash-strapped school could not sustain.[60]

While black schools in South Carolina, like other black southern colleges, benefited during segregation by having the best black players come to their

The Mighty Bulldogs of South Carolina State College, 1953. *Courtesy of W. Eugene Atkinson II, Orangeburg, South Carolina.*

campuses, a few South Carolinians who came out of black high schools left the South and found spots on big schools in the Midwest and elsewhere, where legal segregation did not exist. One of the most notable was J.C. Caroline. A high school star at Columbia's Booker T. Washington, Caroline's notable stats as a quarterback, scoring fifty career touchdowns, reached the notice of Illini coach Ray Eliot. Although he did not offer the Columbia player a scholarship, Eliot invited him to try out as a walk-on. In 1953, his sophomore year, Caroline quickly proved his athletic ability, gaining 204 yards against the mighty Buckeyes of Ohio State and leading the Illini to an upset victory, 41–20. By season's end, Caroline led the nation in rushing with 1,256 yards and gained consensus All-American honors. Ironically, when Caroline came home to Columbia after the season, white leaders of the city honored him with a parade and gifts at Township Auditorium. After two more successful seasons with Illinois, the Chicago Bears drafted Caroline, and he played with them for eleven years as a defensive back.[61]

Other black high school stars who left the South for distinguished college careers included Bill Belk of Lancaster. Starting for Barr Street High in 1963, he helped his school reach the state title game, where they lost to C.A. Johnson of Columbia. Belk took his talent to Maryland State following his high school coach, Sandy Gilliam. There he played with other notable

South Carolinians, including Charleston native Art Shell. In 1968, the San Francisco Forty-Niners made Belk a high draft selection as a tight end. After eight years on the West Coast, Belk retired to his home in South Carolina.[62]

Football Achievements since 1970

Wofford College has seen a somewhat better post-season record than its two small college neighbors, PC and Newberry. Its best years have come in the first decade of the twenty-first century. After Wofford brought back varsity football in 1913, the Terriers had few significant winning seasons, enjoying its occasional victories against its big upstate rival in Greenville and even creating a pennant to commemorate its rare win over Furman in the 1916 contest, 9–7. During the interwar years, the Spartanburg school failed to defeat the Purple Hurricane in nineteen games that extended to 1948 when the two schools tied in that season's contest, 7–7. The following year proved to be one of Wofford's best to that time when it won nine and tied one, that against Furman 13–13. Following the season, the Terriers were invited to the Shriners Cigar Bowl to take on the Florida State Seminoles.

Finalist trophy for the Shriners Cigar Bowl, Tampa, Florida, 1950. As runner-up to Florida State, Wofford received this trophy. It was one of the best years in Terrier football until 2003, when the Spartanburg school played for the I-AA championship. The trophy is displayed at the Wofford Athletic Department. *Courtesy of Susan Dugan, Columbia, South Carolina.*

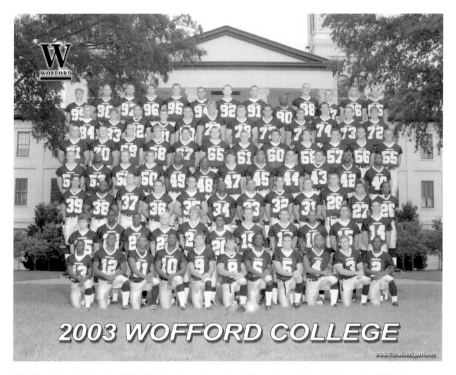

Wofford, finalist in the 2003 I-AA championship. They played the University of Delaware tough in the latter's home state, losing 24–9. This is probably the best year in the school's football history in over three decades. *Courtesy of Wofford Athletics Department, Spartanburg, South Carolina.*

In those early postwar years, when the former Florida teachers college had just begun to allow male students, the future football powerhouse of the Southeast had only had a football team for four years. Consequently, Wofford was heavily favored. Nonetheless, the underdogs from Tallahassee prevailed 19–6. During the 1950s, Wofford had its first winning decade against Furman, going 6-3-1. In the 1968 and 1969 seasons, the two schools had a most unusual two-game series both seasons—in each the Terriers came out victorious. Although these were some of Furman's poorest years in football, they proved two of the best years for Wofford. During the 1970 season, they went on to the NAIA title game against Texas A&I but ran into the best team of the nation, getting humbled 48–7.[63]

In late 1996, the Terriers began to upgrade their program and entered the Southern Conference to compete in the I-AA level. Since the beginning of the new century, Wofford has become one of the Southern Conference's top teams, reaching the I-AA playoffs three times through the 2008 season. In 2003, they made it to the championship game held in Newark, Delaware, where they came up short against the University of Delaware Blue Hens, 24–9.

As it had accomplished in the 1920s and 1930s, Furman has had one of the state's most consistently winning football programs in the last fifty years. Although the Greenville school has suffered through some lean years since 1950, including several losing seasons in the 1950s and '60s, Furman football has rarely had a losing year since the mid-1970s. After Art Baker became head coach in 1973 and laid the foundation for future success, Dick Sheridan began Furman's long run of winning years and several Southern Conference championships. In his first season, Sheridan led the Paladins to their first conference title in 1978, going 8-3 and 4-1 in the conference. Then he directed Furman football to four straight conference titles from 1980 to '83 and its first playoff game in 1982. Although the team lost to South Carolina State College in their first post-season game in Division I-AA, 17–0, this was just the beginning of several playoff appearances in the coming years.

In 1983, Furman defeated Boston University in the first round but then lost a heartbreaker, at home, to Western Carolina, 14–7. Although 1984 was another good year with upset wins over North Carolina State (34–30) and Marshall (38–28), its conference standing declined to fourth place. The next year, Furman almost took the I-AA title but lost an exciting, dramatic contest to Georgia Southern, 44–42, in Tacoma, Washington. It was then that

Furman University Paladin I-AA National Champions, 1988. They defeated Georgia Southern in the final, 17–12, in Pocatello, Idaho. *Courtesy of Furman Athletics Department, Greenville, South Carolina.*

Sheridan was lured away to head up the North Carolina State program. His replacement was assistant Jimmy Satterfield, who took up where Sheridan had left off, culminating in 1988 with the Palmetto State's second national football championship, defeating its old foe from the 1985 title game, Georgia Southern, 17–12, this time in Pocatello, Idaho.[64]

Since the 1988 national title season, Furman has made it to the I-AA final once more, in 2001, losing a close one to Montana, 13–6, under Head Coach Bobby Johnson. It has also won the Southern Conference three more times since 1999, the last time under the direction of Bobby Lamb (2004).[65]

While Furman must rank as one of the state's most consistent small to mid-size college programs during the last thirty years, Clemson and South Carolina still get the most scrutiny from state and national media. With Clemson playing in the state's first college bowl game in the 1940 Cotton Bowl, the Tigers have had the most success both during the regular season and post-season play of any program in the state. Since the formation of the ACC and the first football conference race in 1953, Clemson has taken the conference championship twelve times, the first in 1956 and the last in 1991. But its biggest achievement in college football came following the 1981 season. Under the young head coach, Danny Ford, the Tigers went 11-0 in the regular season and were selected to face perennial national contenders Nebraska in the Orange Bowl on January 1, 1982. Although the Tigers were ranked number one in both national polls leading up to the New Year's Day clash, some sports analysts believed that the Cornhuskers should win even though they were not as strong as past Nebraska teams. While the midwestern school's reputation over the years might have influenced some predictions before the game, the upstate school proved more aggressive and faster on offense and defense, winning the game and the Division I-A National title by a score of 22–15. It was the first national football title in any major college sports program in the state.[66]

Since then, Clemson has tried to regain that national title but without success. While the Tigers have won another five ACC championships since 1981, they have not even been able to play in one of the major bowl games since. After 1991, Clemson has found the competition in the ACC so intense that it has failed to earn another conference championship (as of the end of the 2008 season). With the addition of Florida State to the ACC in 1991, winning the conference title has become more difficult. With further conference expansion announced in 2003, with the addition of Boston College, Virginia Tech and Miami University, the competition for Clemson

Clemson players storm down the hill into "Death Valley," 1988. This tradition prior to every home game has thrilled fans and players alike since Coach Howard introduced it soon after Memorial Stadium was finished. *Courtesy of Clemson University Athletics, Clemson, South Carolina.*

Allen Mitchell behind center during a home game in the 1984 "Black Magic" season when he helped lead the Gamecocks to their best season in their history. *Courtesy of Allen Mitchell, Lexington, South Carolina.*

grew even more intense. However, their longstanding in-state rivalry with South Carolina has usually seen the Tigers dominate. Since 1981, the Tigers have won more than nineteen out of twenty-seven contests over the Gamecocks, giving the upstate school a more than 70 percent winning record during that time period.[67]

As for the Midlands campus, South Carolina has had ambitions similar to its big upstate rivals, but it rarely has had Clemson's success. Perhaps the best season in the last half-century in South Carolina football came in 1984, the legendary Black Magic season. Under Head Coach Joe Morrison, the relatively small but speedy Gamecocks managed a 9-0 start, with notable victories against Notre Dame, in South Bend, and Florida State. While the Gamecocks did defeat Clemson in a close 22–21 contest to end the regular season, their hopes for a number one ranking were dashed by an improbable loss to Navy the week before in Annapolis, 38–21. Although heavily favored to defeat the Midshipmen, Carolina seemed completely unprepared almost from the first whistle. After six turnovers, including two interceptions, the seemingly unbeatable Gamecocks simply could not overcome their own mistakes that day. Their hopes for national prominence ended at the Gator Bowl in a close loss to Oklahoma State, 21–14.[68]

Since that magical season, the Gamecocks have continued to strive for national recognition but rarely have come close to their 1984 achievements. While Joe Morrison led the Gamecocks to back-to-back 8-4 seasons during his last two years as head coach in Columbia, he could never quite reach the level of the Black Magic season. After Morrison's sudden death in early spring of 1989, Carolina experienced several mediocre seasons that became more regular when the school entered the very competitive SEC for the first time in the 1992 season. The worst year in this string came in 1999, the first year that Lou Holtz took on the head coaching duties at Carolina. The excitable, well-traveled Holtz, who had led Notre Dame to the national title in 1989, must have wondered what he had taken over at South Carolina when his first season in Columbia ended 0-11. But then he seemed to turn it completely around, leading the Gamecocks to two thrilling winning seasons, in which they upset a top-ranked Georgia twice in 2000 and 2001 and capped both years with Outback Bowl victories over Ohio State.[69]

The Holtz era then regressed once again, with losing seasons in 2002 and 2003. Although the Gamecocks improved in Holtz's last season with a 6-5 season, in 2004 the big rival game with Clemson at the end of the season put a sad ending to the coach's career when the rivals ended their contest in a brawl on the field at Memorial Stadium in Clemson. The disgraceful performance led the athletic directors at both schools to withdraw their respective sides from bowl consideration that year.[70]

Soon after Holtz's last game, South Carolina made a surprising announcement. Through some secret contacts that began before the end of the football season, Carolina's athletics director, Mike McGee, had pulled off one of the greatest hires in the school's history by signing one of college football's most innovative minds in the modern era, Steve Spurrier. After making Florida into an SEC power during the 1990s, winning seven SEC championships in a little over a decade and one national title, Spurrier had left the college ranks after the 2001 season to try his hand in the NFL as the Washington Redskins' head coach. After two seasons, the former Florida offensive genius found that his magic did not work in the professional ranks, and he resigned. His brief retirement from the game ended with his new team in Columbia with the November 2004 announcement that he was accepting the head coaching job. The Spurrier era that began the following year ended with a 7-5 record and a tough loss to Missouri in the Independence Bowl, 38–31. Since then, Spurrier teams have had some success, finishing at least .500 or better each of the following three seasons but still looking for that breakout year that would emulate the success of Spurrier's Florida Gators from the decade before.[71]

As college football nears the end of its first decade in a new century, the thrill and excitement of every campus seems as strong, if not more so, every fall Saturday as it was half a century ago. Perhaps it is the proliferation of media outlets—numerous sports channels on television, websites on home computers and radio—that magnify football more than was possible when radio and newspapers were the only media. By the 1920s, football had become a fixture of great importance on nearly every campus in the state. Regardless of the budget a school might have, it was important that an institution have a varsity team that could compete against state rivals and even a few beyond the borders of South Carolina.

After World War II, the college ranks began to separate more clearly with respect to competition levels. New conferences such as the Atlantic Coast Conference became the major athletic conferences in which football (along with basketball) predominated because of school interest and the revenue it generated to sustain these major sports and the lesser ones such as track and field and swimming. As television revenue became available and the sports channels began to mushroom in the 1980s, winning became that much more important, if not essential. While high-profile coaches of the 1920s had received generous compensation for their time, today the high-level colleges, demanding wins and championships, must pay coaches the requisite salaries. While some in the public question the huge compensations, far beyond the level received by other members of the college faculty or even high-level college administrators, the pressure to win and the long hours it takes to organize and plan for each Saturday's game provides at least a partial rationale for million-dollar salaries that more and more coaching staffs can now command.

Will this situation be sustainable for the long term? Time will tell. One thing seems clear, though: college football in South Carolina, as in the nation, will remain a fixture in campus life, regardless of the money involved and critics who demand reform. Now let's take a closer look at some of the major personalities and traditional rivalries that have made the game such a significant part of life in the Palmetto State. These traditions and the people who helped to shape them are the essence of why football has become such an emotional, transfixing aspect of life during the last four months of every year.

CHAPTER 4

Integration of College Football

As college football evolved with the growing use of the pass as a major part of the offensive game in the 1960s, a new society began to take shape with the 1954 Supreme Court decision that ruled legal segregation unconstitutional. While its impact only began to affect South Carolina campuses a decade after the decision was proclaimed, it would take even longer to affect college football. Clemson became the first state college to desegregate when Charleston native Harvey Gant began classes on the upstate campus in January 1963. Later that fall, South Carolina admitted its first African American students. Yet it took another seven years for both schools to finally bring in the first African American football players.

Frank Howard observed after he retired from coaching that Clemson was not ready for integrated schools during his tenure on the field. It is difficult to know if Howard would have brought in black players if he thought he could. His famous colleague and fellow Alabama graduate in the 1930s, Paul "Bear" Bryant, wrestled with the same issues during his career at Alabama in the 1960s and early '70s. According to one of his biographers, Bryant wanted to bring black players onto his team much earlier than he actually did. However, due to the political and social makeup of the period, he had to wait until the time was right. Coaches were not social reformers but rather people hired to win football games. Until society was willing to accept black players, all coaches, at least in the South, had to wait for the right moment. In a certain sense, social mores and customs were more important than winning football games until the 1970s.

Bryant signed his first black player in 1970. Other SEC schools did it earlier. The first was Kentucky when it signed a black player in 1965, but most waited another four to five years. And that is when South Carolina college football began to integrate. Coincidence or not, Clemson awarded a scholarship to its first African American player the same year that Alabama had. Marion Reeves came out of Columbia and was discovered when an assistant coach saw some film of Reeves while he was initially scouting a teammate. A solid defensive back, Reeves recalls that one of his best days as a Tiger came against the Gamecocks in 1971 when he made two interceptions to help his team to a 17–7 victory in the annual rivalry. Although his senior year was cut short by a knee injury, Reeves had a brief three-year career in the pros, one year with the Philadelphia Eagles and then two more years with the Winnipeg Blue Bombers of the Canadian Football League. Following his professional career, Reeves came back to Clemson to finish his degree and then began a career in textiles with several firms. He eventually returned to his hometown of Irmo to start his own masonry business. In recent years, he accepted a higher calling to become a pastor.

South Carolina recruited its first African American players one year before Clemson. Carleton Heyward and Ansel E. "Jackie" Brown joined the Gamecocks for the 1969 season. The smaller colleges in the state also recruited their first African Americans at about the same time. Presbyterian College's first black recruit was Sumter High's John Arthur Pressley, but he only stayed for three semesters before leaving. It is not hard to imagine that as the first black player on an all-white team in the early '70s the atmosphere was probably tense, especially when thrust into an unfamiliar surrounding without any friends.

Carl "Elmore" Griffin, a halfback from Thomson, Georgia, was the first African American PC player to graduate in 1976. Elliott Pauling of Elloree, South Carolina, became the first African American at PC to hold a record at the school, leading the team in rushing his last two years. In 1977, Pauling was named to both the NAIA second team All-American squad and received All-Southern Atlantic Conference honors. At the end of the decade, Clayto Burke of Macon, Georgia, earned several records and honors for the PC football team that still stand today. These include most rushing yards (1,575) and top rushing average per game (121.2), both for his senior season in 1979.

By the late 1970s, most colleges in the state were fully integrated, with rosters that were close to half or more African Americans. While the rosters of schools such as Clemson, South Carolina and Presbyterian College have succeeded on the field over the last three decades in large part because of the speed and power of black linemen, wide receivers and running backs, the quarterback position has tended to remain the exclusive right of whites on most teams. But this began to change in the early 1980s. Homer Jordan led Clemson's national title run with his speedy running and deft passing and became the upstate school's first black quarterback. A decade later, one of Wofford's all-time best quarterbacks, Shawn Graves from Marion, South Carolina, set several NCAA Division II records and led the Terriers into the playoffs in 1990 and 1991. At Carolina, Anthony Wright, a Vanceboro, North Carolina high school star, led the Gamecocks for three seasons during the late 1990s. Despite his tremendous abilities as a passer and runner, he was frustrated by injury and, at other times, an uninspired supporting cast. Nonetheless, Wright went on to play quarterback for several NFL teams, including the Dallas Cowboys, the Baltimore Ravens and the New York Giants.

In many ways, the integration of the college game since the early 1970s has transformed football in South Carolina as it has in the rest of the Southeast, not to say the nation. New opportunities that the integration of college football have opened to African Americans provide minorities with more educational opportunities, as well as the chance to play on some of the nation's top programs in the sport. It also gives more minorities better opportunities in the professional ranks, particularly in the NFL, through the better visibility they receive from television and other media outlets. Nonetheless, the fact remains that more often than not black athletes who make it in the college ranks have unrealistic expectations that they can use their college experience to land a big professional contract. Few actually do get that big contract, even though hundreds, perhaps even thousands, think they will. Yet in spite of such statistical realities, most players focus too much on their football skills and neglect the educational opportunities that are provided to them from the athletic scholarships. While it is true that many white athletes have the same professional ambitions as their black counterparts, it is generally also true that white athletes have more opportunities off the football field if they do not make a professional team. Critics have argued that colleges both in South Carolina and the nation as a whole exploit recruits in order to produce a winning team. Once their eligibility is complete, the black athlete has little that can take the place of his dream to be a professional player. However, as long as professional players have the chance to earn large contracts, most talented high school and college players will be hard-pressed to resist the hope of reaching such economic and athletic success.[72]

CHAPTER 5

Special Player Bios

ALEX PREGNALL: COLLEGE OF CHARLESTON STAR, 1910–13

"Pregnall is a broken field runner who picks his openings with the coolness of a veteran." Thus did the young freshman star for the College of Charleston Maroons gain his first noted headline in the Charleston newspaper following the dramatic upset win over their crosstown rivals at The Citadel in October 1910. Alex, a native Charlestonian born in December 1892, became a baseball star for the Charleston High School, which seemed to interest him much more than his academic studies. Although there is no documentation to indicate that he played football for his high school, the ability he showed on the gridiron as a college player suggested that he must have played for the school team as well. Once enrolled at the College, he quickly showed his athletic ability as a runner, kicker and passer. In the 11–0 upset of the cadets, Pregnall orchestrated one of the best tricks of early college football in South Carolina. Many years later, he told his son how he and his teammates fooled the cadet defense for the clinching touchdown. In the huddle, the young freshman instructed the Maroon offense to form a "minor huddle in the backfield" in order to hide Pregnall while he stuffed the ball under his jersey. Then, while his interference headed toward one end of the field, as though they had the ball, Pregnall scampered in the other direction toward the end zone more than sixty yards away. Only after he had gone several yards did The Citadel defense discover the ruse and switch their attention to the speedy runner. They tackled him only four yards from the goal line. But this stop only delayed the inevitable score that came on the next play with Pregnall carrying the ball into the end zone.

Pregnall's play would not be legal today, but even without such trickery the Charleston native became more than a sensation within the ranks of the small student body at the College of Charleston. By 1912, he was the captain of the Maroons and continued to show his football talents both as a runner and punter. Even though the small school lost more games than it won over his career, by the conclusion of the 1912 season, he was named to the "All-South Carolina Team" as the first team quarterback. The only all-star on either the first or second team from the College, he was one of only two other players not from Clemson or Carolina selected that year. The other player was Folger of The Citadel.

Although the all-star is listed on the 1913 Maroons team, it appeared that he did not play much for an unknown reason. Perhaps his need to find work precluded him playing in his last year. Or it might also be that he had had enough of football. Despite his abilities, he preferred baseball because, as he told his son years later, football was so physically punishing to play. Pregnall never graduated but went on to a long career at the nearby Charleston Navy Yard, where he eventually became the head of the design team. But while he did so, he still remained active in both baseball and football, playing on some of the yard teams up to World War I, even helping the yard's Machinist football team to a victory over The Citadel B team in 1913 while also serving as its coach. His baseball career continued, as well, both as a coach of the College of Charleston in 1914 and then as a player and sometime coach of local teams. The former local star kept his hand in sports by officiating high school and college games regularly into the 1930s.

Pregnall's career at the Navy Yard continued into the huge expansion that occurred during World War II. Not long after the war, he was forced to retire due to a heart condition, and he died in 1948.[73]

Dode Phillips

If "what have you done for me lately" had been in vogue for college football in 1921, then David Gardiner "Dode" Phillips would surely be the most admired player in South Carolina football history. On November 18, 1921, Phillips scored the only points as the Erskine College Seceders downed the heavily favored Clemson Tigers by a score of 13–0. He would later be dubbed "King Dodo of Football" in the state, and on that November day,

Phillips gained royalty status forever. Finishing a brilliant four-year career with the Seceders, he scored both touchdowns and kicked the point after to account for all of the points scored that afternoon at Riggs Field in Clemson. In addition to the points scored, Phillips was responsible for most of the rushing yardage for Erskine, as well as completing several key passes and handling all of the kicking duties. He also stood out at linebacker on defense by intercepting two Tiger passes.[74]

Earlier in his senior season, Dode and his teammates had taken the favored Gamecocks of South Carolina to the wire before bowing by a score of 13–7. Phillips ran for a sixty-five-yard touchdown in the fourth period to give the Seceders a 7–6 lead with three minutes left to play. Carolina then marched sixty yards for the winning score, but Dode had created the biggest stir with his impressive run while setting the stage for a stellar season for both him and his Erskine teammates. Two weeks later, Phillips and the Seceders mauled the College of Charleston 74–0 in Due West. Taking on The Citadel the following week, Erskine prevailed with a score of 13–6. Playing before a large crowd at Hampton Park in Charleston, King Dodo again dominated the opposition as he scored both Seceder touchdowns and kicked the extra point. On the opening kickoff, Phillips startled the home crowd by sprinting ninety-five yards for the initial score and then successfully converting to take the lead 7–0. The cadets forged their way back into the game with a second-quarter Antley touchdown to tighten the score to 7–6. Later in the fourth quarter, Phillips intercepted a Citadel aerial and returned it thirty yards for the game-winning touchdown. On October 28, Erskine did battle in Clinton with the Presbyterian College Blue Stockings. In the 21–7 Seceder victory, Dode set up two touchdowns and scored once in the decisive win for Erskine. Phillips and the Seceders ended their storybook season with an overall record of 6-2 that included the before-mentioned games and an opening season loss to Furman and victories over Wofford and Newberry.

Going all the way back to his freshman season in 1917, it was readily apparent that Dode was destined for greatness. In their first game that year, the Seceders edged South Carolina by a score of 14–13. Phillips ran, passed, kicked and backed up the line on defense as Erskine pulled off the upset of the young season. One of his completions in the second period to Blakely for a fifteen-yard touchdown gave the Seceders the early lead. After Carolina tied the score in the third quarter, Phillips threw to end Jakie Todd for a touchdown that covered thirty yards. That pass play lives in Palmetto football lore among all the old-timers as South Carolina's version of Notre

Erskine's 1917 varsity squad went 4-3, including the only time in its nearly half-century of playing the game that the Flying Fleet, then known as the Seceders, defeated South Carolina (14–13). *Sitting, left to right*: Andrew Patrick and Fred Rodgers; *first row, left to right*: Marvin Gault, Jim Bigham, John "Jakie" Todd, Dick Rawls and Lindsey Miller; *second row, left to right*: Bulldog Hagan (Hogan?), Brownlee Stevenson, Dode Phillips, Rube Agnew, Lody Blakely and Frank Quinn; *third row, left to right*: Joe Lindsey, Wade or Hood?, Bostic or Bostwick?, Jim Kennedy, J.D. Hood, Victor Hollis and Coach A.J. Ranson. First names were not available for two of the players. *Courtesy of Coach Cally Gault of Clinton, South Carolina.*

Dame's famed passing tandem of Dorais to Rockne. Rogers kicked both extra points, and Erskine came away with the surprising victory in Dode Phillips's first game as a collegian.

In the four years that Phillips played at Erskine (their schedule was limited to two games in 1918), he was named to the all-state team each year, even as a freshman. His unique abilities on the football field were readily apparent, and his reputation grew each season, culminating with the 1921 season. After that exceptional senior year, he was named to the extremely prestigious All-Southern team that featured players such as Red Roberts and Bo McMillin of Centre, as well as five Georgia Bulldogs and two from Georgia Tech. The *Atlanta Sunday American* wrote:

Phillips of Erskine is a real all-round man. He carried the ball about three out of five times for his team all year, did all the punting, passing, kicking off and kicking goals. He backs up the line for his team in wonderful shape. He slashes on his off-tackle plays with exceptional drive, cuts back very well and is fast in the open. He weighs about 175 pounds and is a beautiful punter. He has scored on every team he has played against this year, though defeated by top heavy scores in some games.

Coach H.J. Stegeman of Georgia made the selections for the newspaper, and for a prominent football coach at a major college like Georgia to recognize Dode Phillips's talent was very impressive. Stegeman failed to observe that all of Erskine's game scores were really close, even the two games that they did not win. But what a way for Phillips to cap off his storied career with the Seceders.

Soon after his graduation from Erskine, Dode became the head coach at Anderson High School prior to returning to his alma mater as the head coach. For the next four years (1924–27), he fashioned an unexpectedly poor record of five wins, twenty-four losses and one tie. That record shows just how exceptional Phillips had been as a player while leading the Seceders to eighteen wins in four years. As a player, he accomplished that feat over the same number of years and against the same caliber of opposition. It is safe to say that there were no more King Dodos out there, and if there were, they did not choose to matriculate in Due West. He was succeeded at Erskine by his current freshman coach and ex-teammate, Jakie Todd, who stayed with the Seceders, then the Flying Fleet, until 1940. After his brief coaching career at Erskine, Phillips played a season of minor league baseball before taking over as head coach at the Moultrie High School in Georgia, where he coached through the 1935 season.

Dode then entered the insurance business in Greenville for the next three years, prior to returning to Due West to assist his old friend Jakie Todd. He served as the freshman coach for two years in addition to his duties as a special ambassador for the college. Dode then assumed the position of supervisor of physical education for the South Carolina Department of Education, as well as heading up the American Legion Junior Baseball program in the state. After that, he became an executive with several pharmaceutical companies before returning to Erskine in 1962 to serve as the director of admissions.

Phillips continued to garner acclaim long after his playing days with the Seceders had ended. He was presented the Service to Sports Award by the Atlantic Coast Conference Sportswriters Association in 1958 and was inducted into the South Carolina Athletic Hall of Fame as a charter member two years later. A little more than two weeks before he succumbed to his second heart attack, Dode was inducted into the National Association of Intercollegiate Athletics Hall of Fame. David Gardiner Phillips passed away on December 29, 1965, at the age of sixty-six, still being called "Mr. Football" in South Carolina.[75]

Banks McFadden: First All-American in Palmetto State College Football, 1939

Perhaps one of the state's best all-around athletes of all time, Banks McFadden developed his skills at Great Falls, South Carolina, where he starred in several sports. A great runner and passer, he entered Clemson in 1936 and soon became an integral part of the football team, but his athletic skills were much farther reaching than the gridiron. He also led the varsity basketball team and starred in varsity track in the spring. While he led the Tigers to their first bowl game in 1940, he also helped the basketball team to its only Southern Conference championship the previous year. While being an integral part of the Clemson offense for three years through his speedy running and deft passing and kicking, McFadden also played a tough defensive game, often stopping the run with crunching tackles from the linebacker position. He played key roles in the Tigers' victories in the annual Big Thursday game in 1937 and 1939, gaining valuable yards on the ground and throwing key passes for big gains, as well as kicking extra points. He still holds one of the longest yards from scrimmage runs in Clemson football history, sprinting ninety yards against PC in the 1939 contest.

As his senior year wound up on the football field, honors never before experienced by a football player in the Palmetto State started to roll in. Named to the first team All-America squad that year, the Great Falls native was also selected as "America's Most Versatile Athlete" by the Associated Press and later became a member of the College Football Hall of Fame. Clemson did not overlook his great abilities, either. He is a member of the school's All-Time Football Team and is one of only three Clemson players to have his number retired.

After graduating in 1940, McFadden was drafted by the Brooklyn Dodgers. In his rookie season, he led all runners in total yardage and seemed headed for an all-pro career. Unfortunately, a severe car crash in the off-season back in South Carolina caused a knee injury and ended his professional career.

Clemson All-American Banks McFadden hurdles a Presbyterian College tackler in a 1939 game. *Courtesy of Presbyterian College Archives, Clinton, South Carolina.*

After serving in World War II, McFadden returned to his alma mater to serve as an assistant under Coach Howard while also coaching the Clemson basketball team for several seasons. Still admired by the Clemson faithful as one of its best all these years later, McFadden passed away in 2003.[76]

LOU SOSSAMON: THE UNIVERSITY OF SOUTH CAROLINA'S FIRST ALL-AMERICAN, 1942

A Gaffney, South Carolina native who starred for his local high school as one of the best linemen in the state, Lou Sossamon chose South Carolina, where he anchored the Gamecocks' line from 1940 to 1942. During his college career, he helped end Clemson's seven-year dominance of the Big Thursday game with an 18–14 victory in 1941. He also led the Carolina squad against a top Tennessee team in the first game of the 1942 season in which the Gamecocks battled the Volunteers to a 0–0 tie. The only blemish of sorts suffered by the Knoxville school that season, they went on to the Sugar Bowl in January. During his senior year, Sossamon stood out enough—despite his team's sub-par season at 1-7-1—to be selected by the Associated Press to its second team All-American squad.

Soon after his graduation, Sossamon entered the U.S. Navy to serve his country in World War II, but his football talents came in handy. He helped lead the Bainbridge Naval Station's football team to one of the best records in armed forces football in 1944 and 1945 at center. Once his military service ended, he signed a contract with the New York Yankees of the All-American Football Conference, a short-lived professional league that lasted until 1950. Sossamon had a three-year career with the Yankees and helped them reach the finals of the league playoffs twice, although they lost both to the Cleveland Browns. Unlike today, where professional players in the NFL sign huge contracts, Sossamon had what then was considered a good annual professional contract of $8,000, which was supplemented with playoff bonus money. But after three years, he returned to Gaffney permanently to help his father run the local *Gaffney Ledger*, which he eventually bought to become the publisher until his retirement in the 1990s. Along with a stellar publishing career, Sossamon served on the University of South Carolina Board of Trustees for several years. He was also inducted into the University of South Carolina Hall of Fame and is a member of the South Carolina Athletic Hall of Fame. He is now retired and lives in West Columbia.[77]

Doc Blanchard

Even though Felix Anthony "Doc" Blanchard only played one season of high school football in the Palmetto State, he is nonetheless revered as one of the state's all-time greatest players. Born to Felix Anthony "Big Doc" and Mary Tatum Blanchard in McColl on December 11, 1924, his family moved to Dexter, Iowa, soon after. They resided in Dexter for nine years prior to moving to Bishopville. Doc attended Bishopville Grammar School and Bishopville High School, where he played one year of football as an eighth grader before enrolling at St. Stanislaus Academy in Bay St. Louis, Mississippi. His innate football-playing ability and athleticism can be traced to Big Doc, who played at both Tulane University in his native Louisiana and at Wake Forest College near Raleigh, North Carolina.

According to Doc himself, when he first began his career at Bishopville High, their first opponent was a strong Bennettsville High team, and they were having trouble holding the score down. Doc was inserted at linebacker, and Bennettsville immediately ran a play over him for a touchdown. But later in the game, he made his first tackle, and few teams were ever able to run touchdowns over him again. The next season (1938) found him at St. Stanislaus, his father's alma mater, where he played for Arthur "Slick"

Morton, who would later become the head coach at Southeastern Louisiana College, VMI and Mississippi State University. Doc achieved national acclaim while at St. Stanislaus and became the target for college football coaches nationwide. National powerhouses such as Notre Dame, Tulane and Fordham all coveted the highly touted Blanchard. Along with his dad, Doc chose the University of North Carolina, where his mother's cousin, "Sunny Jim" Tatum, was the head coach. He played freshman football in 1942 at North Carolina, since first-year players were still ineligible for varsity competition. His reputation as a gridiron star continued to escalate around the country, even as a non-varsity player.[78]

With World War II at hand, Doc put his football career aside in April 1943 when he was drafted into the air force. After serving for fourteen months doing

FIFTEEN CENTS   NOVEMBER 12, 1945

TIME

THE WEEKLY NEWSMAGAZINE

JUNIOR DAVIS & DOC BLANCHARD
They make Army's T look.
(Sport)

VOLUME XLVI   NUMBER 20

preparatory work at Lafayette College in Pennsylvania, Doc earned an appointment to West Point and immediately began to concentrate on conditioning for a different type of warfare—on the gridiron. On October 1, 1944, Doc Blanchard finally played his first college football game. He scored a touchdown in his debut as the Cadets swamped an outmanned but game North Carolina eleven by the score of 46–0. A couple of weeks later, Doc and his teammates administered the worst defeat ever on the Pitt Panthers with a 69–7 thrashing. He scored two touchdowns as the Cadets repaid the Panthers, who dominated the army gridders during their 1930s heyday. A hard-fought 27–7 triumph over the Duke Blue Devils at the Polo Grounds in New York City gave West Point an unblemished 5-0 slate to begin Doc's initial season on the Hudson.

During the 1945 season, Doc Blanchard (right) and his fellow running back Glenn Davis had become household names throughout the nation. This November 1945 *Time* issue shows the celebrity status that they had achieved that season. Soon after the release of this issue, Blanchard was awarded the Heisman Trophy, the first earned by a South Carolina native. His partner earned it the following season. *Courtesy of John Daye, Irmo, South Carolina.*

Two weeks later, the Cadets unleashed their offensive fury on Notre Dame at Yankee Stadium with a resounding 59–0 thumping. It had been thirteen years since Army had experienced victory over the Irish. With Doc being used as a decoy and a blocker, the large stable of Cadet running backs ran wild all afternoon. Head Coach Earl "Red" Blaik admitted early in the season that no other team, college or pro, could boast of as many quality backs as the Cadets were able to employ in 1944. After a lopsided tune-up against the Penn Quakers, the Cadets got down to business for their annual clash against the Midshipmen of the Naval Academy at Baltimore's Memorial Stadium. Doc and teammate Glenn Davis provided the firepower as the Army team prevailed 23–7 against the rugged Midshipmen. It was the first West Point victory over its rivals in five long years. Also at stake was an opportunity for its first undefeated season since the 1916 campaign, as well as national championship honors. As was almost always the case, Doc was at his best in the big games, and the 1944 Navy game was no exception with his great all-round play against the Middies that day.

Doc's second season at West Point was more of the same, with another undefeated season and more individual achievements for the burly fullback from Bishopville. During the 1945 campaign, Doc and Glenn registered twenty-three running plays of forty-eight yards or more. Between the two superstars-to-be, they tallied thirty-seven touchdowns, with Blanchard amassing nineteen and Davis eighteen. Add an extremely talented quarterback (Arnold Tucker) and emerging star running backs (Rip Rowan and Shorty McWilliams), and another eminently successful season was on the horizon. Even though their interior linemen were not quite as daunting as the 1944 group, the ends were two of the best—Barney Poole and Hank Foldberg. After two relatively easy season-opening wins against Army Air Force Personnel Distribution Center and Wake Forest, the Cadets took on the Wolverines of Michigan in a nationally prominent contest. Doc ran for two touchdowns as Army outlasted the Big Ten powerhouse by a score of 28–7 at Yankee Stadium.

Two more one-sided victories led to the annual Army–Notre Dame clash at Yankee Stadium in November. With Blanchard and Davis leading the way again, the Cadets handily disposed of the Irish with a convincing 48–0 triumph. As Coach Blaik was quoted later, when the Irish and the Cadets get together, no quarter is given, and big scores are garnered by whichever team can get them. Two weeks later, with over 100,000 spectators present at Philadelphia's Municipal Stadium, Doc scored three touchdowns to pace Army to a 32–13 season-ending victory over the Midshipmen. Not only did he assure the Cadets their second consecutive undefeated season and second national championship, but Doc also wrapped up the race for the highly coveted Heisman Trophy with his performance that day. Thus the small Pee Dee town of Bishopville assumed its place in the sporting world's spotlight in January when Doc was awarded the prestigious award signifying the best in college football. In addition to the Heisman, he was also named the winner of the Walter Camp Award, which denoted the top player in the country.

Early in the first half in the season opener against Villanova, Doc experienced his first serious football injury and was forced to sit out the remainder of that game and the entire game the next two weeks. Although the Cadets prevailed against Villanova, Oklahoma and Cornell, they struggled offensively in all three games. Doc returned for the Michigan game and played almost the whole game as Army continued to struggle offensively in the narrow 20–13 win in Ann Arbor. Getting back in sync the following week with a 48–14 pasting of the undefeated Columbia Lions, Blanchard and company rolled to an insurmountable 28–0 halftime lead. Two consecutive shutout wins against Duke and West Virginia led to the "Game of the Century" against the Irish of Notre Dame at Yankee Stadium. Doc and Tucker provided the defensive leadership as the two powerhouses fought to an unusual scoreless tie to provide the only blemish on the Cadets' three-year slate. Refusing to bow to the extreme pressures of three years with no losses, Army responded the next week with Blanchard leading the way against a much-improved Penn eleven as the Cadets blasted the Quakers by a score of 34–7. Even though Navy came into the annual military skirmish against the Cadets with only one win, Army should have been wary with the public giving the Middies almost no chance to win. The Cadets jumped out to a 21–6 halftime lead and had to hold off Navy at their own five-yard line on the last play of the game to pull off their twenty-seventh victory against only one tie in three years. Never again would two players such as Blanchard and Davis accomplish what they did individually in addition to their twenty-eight-game non-losing streak.

During the winter of their senior year, Doc, Glenn and Barney were offered sizable guaranteed contracts to play professional football. It was estimated that they would receive up to $50,000 each. All three applied for four-month furloughs in order to be available for the upcoming pro football season. The furloughs were categorically denied for each player by Pentagon officials. Doc successfully ended his playing career in Chicago at the fourteenth annual college all-star game against the professional Chicago Bears. In one of the most significant upsets of the series, the all-stars shut out the Bears 16–0 with Doc starting in his customary fullback position.[79]

Doc received his silver wings as a fighter plane pilot at the Williams Air Force Base in Arizona in October 1948 and immediately embarked on an air force career that spanned over thirty years. He was stationed on such bases across the country as Williams AFB, Shaw AFB, Steward AFB, Luke AFB, Tyndall AFB and Randolph Field. In 1960, Doc assumed command of the Third Air Force's Seventy-seventh Tactical Fighter Squadron at Weathersfield in England. His leadership and expertise as an air force pilot far outweighed his superb athletic accomplishments and should be duly noted.

He passed away on April 19, 2009, in Bulverde, Texas, at the age of eighty-four. Doc and the former Jody King were married for forty-five years until her death in 1993. Survivors include his children, Tony, Josephine and Resa, as well as his sister, Mary Elizabeth of Sumter.

CHAPTER 6

Famous Coaches of the Palmetto State

John W. Heisman:
The First Coaching Legend in South Carolina

A Cleveland, Ohio native born in 1869, John Heisman grew up in Titusville, Pennsylvania, where his father made a good living at making and repairing barrels for the then budding oil industry in that area. Initially enrolled at Brown University in 1887, Heisman became a skillful baseball player and also played on the club football squad. After one year, he transferred to the University of Pennsylvania, where he studied law and became a part of the Penn varsity football squad. Though he received his law degree in 1892, he chose to devote his career to the evolving new profession of football coaching. He started at Oberlin College in Ohio, but within a couple of seasons, he was attracted to Auburn, Alabama, to develop its young team.

Then, in 1900, Clemson lured him to the upstate school to develop its varsity squad that had only started playing football three years before. Heisman's genius in football coaching grew out of his willingness to innovate and find new formations to open up the game. He had already begun to view the forward pass as one way to make the game more wide open, but he could not get the "Father of Football," Walter Camp, to accept this innovation until after he left South Carolina. Nonetheless, he took the talent he had at Clemson and in four brief years made it into one of the strongest in the Southeast region.

The year before he arrived, the Tigers were 4-2, but in his first season Heisman took the Tigers to an undefeated season. This included four shutout victories, including a 51–0 triumph over South Carolina, as well as big wins over Alabama (35–0) and Georgia (39–5). The Heisman shift that he would perfect later probably began to take shape during his short four-year tenure at Clemson. The young coach taught his line to shift its position in the line just prior to the snap so that the defenders were completely off balance when the play began, often allowing his running back to burst through the line for big gains. He also used ruses against his opposition before some games. Prior to the 1902 contest against Georgia Tech, the crafty coach sent a group of Clemson cadets into Atlanta to live it up and cause Tech officials and supporters to see them. Thinking this was the football team debauching themselves, the local officials thought they might have a good chance the next day against the upstate college. Unbeknownst to Tech was that Heisman's real team had stayed in a small town north of Atlanta the night before the match. Once they came the next day to play, they easily defeated the overconfident opposition, 44–5. In Heisman's last year at Clemson, he led the school to the Southern Intercollegiate Athletic Association final versus Cumberland College, considered in its day the title game for the southern regional championship. The Montgomery, Alabama match ended in an 11–11 tie.

Because of his success, other schools sought his services, especially those that lost to him. Georgia Tech, having lost to Clemson in 1903, lured the football innovator to Atlanta, where he quickly transformed that team into a regional power. Offering him an annual salary of $2,250 plus 30 percent of the gate, after expenses, it was easy for Heisman to leave Clemson, where he was making $1,800. After Tech's 73–0 loss to Clemson during Heisman's last year in the upstate, the new coach in Atlanta reversed the fortunes of his new college in his first year, holding the Tigers to an 11–11 tie.

Heisman directed Tech to fifteen winning seasons that saw his charges win several conference titles and dominate its biggest in-state rival, the University of Georgia, through World War I. As for Clemson, once Heisman left, it took more than three decades for it to regain its dominant position. Although the Tigers did manage to beat Heisman's Atlanta squad twice following that initial tie, after 1907 Georgia Tech defeated the upstate school ten times without defeat or a tie through 1919 (the two schools did not play each other from 1915 to 1917). An example of how powerful Tech's offense became under Heisman was demonstrated in 1916, when they overwhelmed Cumberland College of Kentucky, 222–0, the biggest score in collegiate football history.

While leading Tech to prominence, Heisman continued to develop innovative formations and worked with other coaches and administrators of the game to open up the offense, creating plays that became instrumental to the game we know so well. These innovations included the center snap, the hidden ball play and the Heisman shift (the forerunner to the T and I formation) mentioned above. However, his lasting impact on the game was his promotion and development of the forward pass. Heisman had tried to have the forward pass adopted before 1906, arguing that it could open up the game and make it more exciting. He opposed the restrictions placed on the passing game when it was first adopted. He worked to abolish the original rule that stated that an incompleted pass automatically reverted to the defending team, whether the incompletion was on a first or fourth down. He also opposed the early passing rule requiring that the passer be at least five yards behind the line of scrimmage to pass the ball and that the pass could be no longer than twenty yards.

His stand went against the legendary Walter Camp, who only reluctantly accepted the forward pass in 1906 and did all he could to maintain the restrictions placed on its use after that. As the pass was debated and argued over and over in the off-season up to World War I, Heisman continued to lobby the reluctant Camp to relax his restrictions. Like all innovators, Heisman's revisions took time to be implemented, but before he retired from coaching in 1927, most of his reforms had been adopted. How amazed he would be by how his ideas have been adapted in the modern era in which the pass has become such an integral part of every game in the last several decades.

After World War I, Heisman left Tech, returning north to coach. He had brief tenures at the University of Pennsylvania (1920–23) and then one season at Washington and Jefferson before his final three years back in the South coaching Rice. When he retired in 1927, his record of 187 wins, 68 losses and 18 ties made him one of the greats of the first half-century of college football. In his retirement, Heisman moved to New York City, opening a sporting goods store and operating the Downtown Athletic Club. From here the first annual award for the best college football player east of the Mississippi was selected in 1935, originally named the DAC trophy (for Downtown Athletic Club). Heisman died in October 1936, just a few weeks before the second award was announced. By the time the trophy was awarded, it was renamed in his memory as the Heisman Memorial Trophy, something that all fans and players of the game know so well today.[80]

Billy Laval: Furman, South Carolina and Newberry Head Coach

It has been said that Billy Laval "took his'n and beat your'n, then took your'n and beat his'n." That old football adage was supposedly coined by Clemson's Frank Howard when Tom Nugent moved from Florida State in 1958 to Maryland. Nugent had beaten Maryland the year before and in his first season at Maryland returned the favor for the Terps. Laval did it first and did it more convincingly than any other football coach in history. He was the head coach at Furman from early in the 1915 season until 1927, when he was employed by the University of South Carolina to head up its athletic department and coach the football team. From 1921 through 1927, Laval and his Hurricane beat South Carolina's Gamecocks six times while losing only once. After taking the reins in Columbia, his Carolina teams beat Furman four times, lost twice and tied on one occasion. Probably no other coach in history has been as successful as Laval was on either side of the coaching fence back in the early days of collegiate football.

Billy Laval graduated from Furman in 1904 after a stellar career as a baseball player and then gravitated to North Carolina A&M (North Carolina State) and played another baseball season in 1905. It was then that Laval embarked on an unusual path in becoming a very innovative college football coach. Sandwiched between seven seasons of minor league baseball, he was the baseball coach at Erskine (twice), Sewanee and Furman for a total of eight seasons. In the fall of 1914, Laval became an assistant football coach for the first time when he assisted W.B. Bible at Furman. He then took over as the head coach in 1915 after the first game of the year, staying in that position for the next thirteen seasons. Until Dick Sheridan and Jimmy Satterfield became Furman head coaches in the latter part of the century, no other coaches were able to match or surpass Laval's thirteen-year record at Furman. His eighty-eight wins are still tops on Furman's all-time coaching list, and his winning percentage of .688 remains the all-time third best. More importantly, Laval coached the game with imagination and flair along with some innovative offensive ideas and strategies that were well ahead of the times.

After Coach Bible's 94–0 loss to Clemson in the opening game in 1915, Laval assumed command and immediately defeated Erskine by a score of 60–0 to burst onto the coaching scene. He went on to win four more and lose twice to effectively set the tone for the remainder of his career in Greenville. During the remainder of the World War I era, Laval and Furman suffered through three losing seasons before commencing on an outstanding nine-year run, beginning in 1919 and ending in 1927, with a brilliant 10-1 record and eventually seven mythical state championships. According to Furman's football media guide, several achievements and milestones marked that early reign for Laval and Furman. In 1916, Laval was responsible for wooing Harold "Speedy" Speer from Winston-Salem, North Carolina, to the Furman campus with the assistance of a group of Greenville citizens. Those citizens raised enough money to pay Speer's tuition, making him the first recruited player in Furman football history.

That same year, William Gressette scored a school record of five touchdowns in another resounding win over Erskine, 60–3. The 1918 season produced a dubious milestone for Furman football, with Georgia Tech administering the worst defeat in school history. Coach John Heisman, formerly head coach at Clemson, led the Atlantans to a 118–0 thrashing of the Purple Hurricane. After that season, it was all downhill for Furman and Laval. A 13–0 win over Oglethorpe University in 1919 served as the dedication game for the new Furman playing facility named Manly Field, and a 7–7 tie with arch rival Clemson catapulted the Laval men to their first acknowledged state collegiate football championship.

A hard-fought 7–0 loss to Georgia was the only blemish on the 1920 slate for the Purple Hurricane as they garnered their second consecutive state championship with a 9-1 record. The following season, Furman finished strong with five consecutive wins to claim its third state championship in succession. A scoreless tie with Clemson and a 7–0 triumph over the Gamecocks spearheaded the run that ended with a 7-2-1 mark. An eight-win season in 1922 in addition to a nine-win season in 1923 were both marred with losses to South Carolina (7–27) and Clemson (6–7), respectively. Those losses effectively eliminated the Purple Hurricane from state championship contention those two years. Then Laval and Furman forged a four-year stranglehold on the championship trophy, beginning in 1924 when they laid claim to a share of the championship with the Gamecocks. The newly awarded FOCUS Cup was presented to both Furman and Carolina that first year as the Hurricane lost to The Citadel while shutting out the Gamecocks and Tigers. With crucial victories over The Citadel, South Carolina and Clemson, Laval and the Hurricane reclaimed their familiar spot alone at the top of the Palmetto State standings in 1925. For the second successive season, all but one of their losses came from out-of-state foes, as they continued their dominance over in-state colleges. Two extremely successful campaigns followed in 1926 and 1927 for the Laval-led Furman team, as they finished with 8-1-1 and 10-1 slates while winning two more state titles. After an impressive 14–7 victory over Georgia in 1926, the Hurricane suffered their only loss in 1927 to their interstate rivals by a score of 32–0. Laval's charges defeated Carolina for the fifth consecutive season, as well as bested Clemson for the fourth time in succession in Laval's final fling as Furman's mentor. A.P. "Dizzy" McLeod, who captained Laval's 1922 squad, was named to succeed the venerable Laval after he bolted to Columbia with his target-faced jerseys and "Crazy Quilt" offense.[81]

Laval hit the field running in Columbia as he opened his inaugural 1928 season in Columbia with five straight wins, including a highly improbable 6–0 road win over Big Ten powerhouse Chicago and its legendary coach, Amos Alonzo Stagg. Carolina's student newspaper reported that thirty-five thousand attended the game in Chicago, with many of those Chicago fans eventually rooting for the Gamecocks and their pleasing style of play. Ed Zobel's stellar punting and running were key elements in the victory, as well as Julian Beall's overall line play. Several times during the game, Stagg used four different players to combat Beall and his aggressive play, but to no avail. His "his'n-your'n" triumph over Furman highlighted his first year at Carolina as the Gamecocks finished with a respectable 6-2-2 mark. Carlisle Beall's seventy-three-yard pass to Bru Boineau provided the only score as Carolina defeated the Hurricane for the first time in six years. The lopsided loss to Clemson on Big Thursday and scoreless ties with The Citadel in Orangeburg and North Carolina spoiled an otherwise successful debut for Coach Laval in the capital city. That first year would prove to be the high mark of his seven seasons with the Gamecocks. He never suffered a losing season but was never able to accomplish the breakthrough campaign that would solidify his tenure and propel his teams to greater heights.

The ensuing two seasons produced six wins each year but were filled with disappointments for the Gamecocks. Losses both years to Clemson were tempered with another Laval victory over his alma mater while experiencing losses to Florida and Tennessee. Along with the Clemson loss in 1930 came Laval's first loss to Furman, but as usual he inspired the Gamecocks to a monumental upset win over nationally recognized LSU by a score of 7–6. Miles Blount notched the lone Carolina touchdown, and Boineau provided the eventual game-winning point after. Laval's second major success over a national power had Gamecock supporters and administrators initiating conversations concerning a reasonably large stadium that would replace the small, antiquated Melton Field.

The talk concerned the construction of at least a thirty-thousand-seat edifice that would more than adequately supplant the harshly unaccommodating

Melton Field. It would be several years before the new structure would become a reality, but Laval and his troops continued their winning ways during the interim period. Gaffney's version of the "Galloping Ghost," Earl Clary, became eligible for the first time in 1931, and the next three years were filled with excitement and anticipation albeit fewer wins than expected. Clary was the first running back in school history to record as many as four 100-yard games, but nagging injuries reduced his effectiveness throughout his three-year career. Nevertheless, there were several triumphant games for the Clary-led Gamecocks. One game worth mentioning was the Clemson game of 1931 that featured first-year Clemson assistant Frank Howard. In that particular game, Clary amassed 147 yards to lead Carolina to a convincing 21–0 victory that had the young Howard remarking that "a fella as good as Clary had no business being on the opposite side of the field." Clary again provided the impetus in victories over The Citadel and Furman but injured a knee in the 6–6 tie with Florida and never regained his effectiveness that season.

New stadium talk filled the air again in 1932 as Laval and the Gamecocks sprinted out to a 3-1 record. As in the previous season, Clary suffered another nagging injury that curtailed his ability as an offensive threat. This time it was an ankle sprain against Wake Forest. As usual, Clary recovered and responded well in the Clemson game in which he dealt Clemson another loss with both timely running and well-thrown passes. Another Furman loss dampened the fans' enthusiasm, but a 20–20 tie with Southern Conference power Auburn helped alleviate the pain. Mediocrity resulted once again with the 5-4-2 final record. The 1933 season proved to be somewhat of an improvement with Clary once more in an on-again, off-again mode due to injuries. Two early season losses to a Pop Warner–coached Temple team and an excellent Villanova eleven had the Gamecock supporters really concerned. But Laval and his Clary-led contingent responded with mid-season victories against Clemson, The Citadel and Virginia Tech to move their record to 4-2. After a one-sided loss in Baton Rouge, the Gamecocks finished with a win over NC State in Columbia, a scoreless tie with always tough Furman and an impressive 16–14 upset over Auburn. Clary was healthy at the end of the season and was instrumental in the Auburn upset, as well as the victory against NC State prior to the Furman tie. With all of the injuries suffered by the Gaffney Ghost, both he and the Gamecocks remained really competitive and finished with a better-than-average 6-3-1 final in 1933.

Finally, all of the stadium talk became a reality in 1934 as the Gamecocks opened the new eighteen-thousand-seat Municipal Stadium with a rain-soaked 22–6 victory over VMI. Even with the graduation of Clary and a talented senior class, Laval and his band of Gamecocks played well throughout the season. After two early season victories, Carolina lost to the likes of NC State, Clemson, Villanova and Washington and Lee while taking care of business against Virginia Tech, The Citadel and Furman. Laval's contract as head football coach and supervisor of all coaches ended after the 1934 season. University officials opted not to renew his contract, and the "Crazy Quilt" era of Carolina football was over. Laval finished his tenure in Columbia without a losing season while notching thirty-nine victories, but he struggled against Clemson with three wins and four losses. It has been said that with a completely healthy "Ghost," the greatness so clamored for by Gamecock faithful could have been achieved and Laval would have survived.[82]

While taking the 1935 season off from coaching football, he became the southern scout for the Boston Red Sox, thus rekindling his love for baseball. In 1936, he was hired as head football coach by Emory and Henry College in Bristol, Virginia, where he stayed for two seasons. Although Laval won only four games in those two seasons, he was gradually rebuilding the moribund program and actually recorded wins over Appalachian, Newberry and Presbyterian in his second season there. Those successes were evidently enough to impress the Newberry College administration, as Laval was offered and accepted the Indians' coaching job for the 1938 season. Thus he became the only coach in South Carolina football history to have served as the head coach at three different Palmetto State colleges.

When Laval took over at Newberry, the Indians were coming off a three-year stretch in which they had won only four games. He immediately led Newberry to twenty-five victories in his first five seasons, including a sterling 7-2-1 record in his third season. Their two losses were to Appalachian State and VMI, as well as a 6–6 tie with Elon, while the Indians downed in-state rivals Erskine, Wofford and Presbyterian in addition to Carson-Newman, Lenoir-Rhyne, Oglethorpe and High Point. That 1940 season was the second-best in school history at the time, trailing only the 1924 team that finished with an 8-2 overall record. The Indians remained competitive until the World War II seasons of 1943 and 1944. After the war, Laval responded with a glowing 6-1 record in 1945 as Newberry defeated Guilford, Mars Hill and Presbyterian, as well as the "B" teams from South Carolina (2) and Georgia. After that season, the postwar years were not kind to the coach known as "the Fox." Averaging only three wins per year from 1946 to 1949, as well as battling an illness, Laval stepped down after the 1949 season, thus ending thirty-two years at three schools that netted him 168 Palmetto State victories.

Laval spent two years in baseball as president of the Palmetto Baseball League in Florence and as general manager of the minor league Greenwood Tigers prior to going into business in Newberry. He died at the home of his daughter in Columbia on January 20, 1957, at the age of seventy-two.[83]

REX ENRIGHT:
SOUTH CAROLINA'S GENTLEMAN COACH

After an illustrious career as a fullback at Notre Dame and a two-year stint with the Green Bay Packers, Rex Edward Enright embarked on a collegiate coaching career that would include stops at the University of North Carolina, the University of Georgia and finally at the University of South Carolina. While at Notre Dame, Enright had two quality seasons. In 1923, he was a reserve fullback who scored touchdowns in victories over Kalamazoo College and Purdue. An injury forced him to miss the entire 1924 season, which was the year of the famed "Four Horsemen" and the "Seven Mules." Enright returned to action in 1925 as the starting fullback for the 7-2-1 Irish. He and quarterback Christy Flanagan led the charge against such powerhouses as Minnesota and Georgia Tech, utilizing Enright's power thrusts and Flanagan's speed. His best day at fullback was against Carnegie Tech when he carried twenty-eight times for 125 yards and two touchdowns. In the Northwestern game, he carried the ball eight out of fourteen consecutive plays to net the Irish two touchdowns in eight minutes. Capping off his stellar season, Enright was named to Walter Eckersall's All-Western Eleven for 1925. Headlining that year's best in the west were such legends as Red Grange, Benny Friedman, Bennie Oosterbaan and La Vern Dilweg to go along with Enright, who was cited by Eckersall as the most valuable player on Knute Rockne's eleven.

Following his graduation in 1926, Enright spent the next two seasons with the NFL's Green Bay Packers. Playing in nineteen games over a two-year span, Enright is credited by NFL record-keepers with scoring five rushing touchdowns for the Packers. Curly Lambeau, the founder/head coach/best player, led the Packers along with future hall of famers Verne Lewellen and Dilweg during this era. In December 1927, Enright and teammate Pid Purdy were persuaded to join the Portsmouth Shoe-Steels for a game against Ashland. Portsmouth was headed by player/coach Jim Thorpe and was constantly signing "ringers" for each game. Unfortunately, Enright and Purdy were involved in an automobile accident en route to Portsmouth and never played again in the NFL. Enright's playing career ended that day in December, and his coaching career was about to commence full time.

Chuck Collins, a former teammate at Notre Dame and then head football coach at the University of North Carolina, hired Enright as a football assistant in the spring of 1928. Enright had previously served as an assistant coach at the American College of Physical Education in Chicago while playing with the Packers. After serving for four seasons in Chapel Hill as the freshman coach, Enright was lured to the University of Georgia by another Notre Dame teammate, Harry Mehre, as an assistant football and head basketball coach. In something of an irony, it was Mehre who interviewed with the athletic committee at South Carolina in late December 1937, with Enright accompanying him to Columbia. After being named to the post in Columbia, Enright was still the Georgia basketball coach but soon handed most of the duties to eventual Carolina assistant Vernon "Catfish" Smith for the remainder of the season. His six-year basketball record at Georgia was 62-54 (.534).[84]

Assembling a coaching staff was the first order of business for the new Gamecock head coach early in 1938. He brought two of his fellow assistants from the Mehre staff, line coach Ted Twomey and end coach Smith. They were joined by a recent graduate of Michigan, Ted Petoskey, who would coach the freshman team. Another piece of business was the terms of the contract for the new mentor. Dr. J. Rion McKissick, along with the athletic committee member Sol Blatt, announced that Enright would receive a four-year deal worth $5,500 per year. The previous head coach, Don McCallister, who had recently resigned as head coach, would be paid the $4,000 called for in his contract, which ran until December 31, 1938.[85]

Enright's initial season in Columbia was his best of the first five. Carving out a respectable 6-4-1 mark in 1938 gave the Gamecock faithful reason for optimism. His schedules during the pre–World War II years were among the toughest and most diverse of any team in the old Southern Conference. Some of the prewar teams that showed up on Carolina's schedules were Xavier (Ohio), Georgia (4), Villanova (2), Duquesne (2), Fordham, Catholic University (2), Florida, Miami (Florida) (4), Penn State, Kansas State (2), Tennessee and Alabama, in addition to traditional conference foes Clemson, Wake Forest, West Virginia, Furman, The Citadel and North Carolina.

Close back-to-back one-point losses to Georgia and Wake Forest, as well as a hard-fought 13–0 loss to eastern powerhouse Fordham, kept the Gamecocks from national prominence in Enright's first season in Columbia. Fordham was coached by Enright's old Notre Dame teammate and roommate, Sleepy

Jim Crowley, making the loss even more difficult. Future Green Bay Packer Larry Craig, Al Grygo and Dick Little were the catalysts in that near-miss season of 1938. A lopsided 34–12 loss on Big Thursday to the Clemson Tigers was the first of four losses to their in-state rivals prior to World War II. A prime example of Enright's penchant for constructing really tough schedules came in 1941 when Carolina won four, lost none and tied one in conference play. His first win over Clemson was the highlight of that season along with a 0–0 tie with Peahead Walker's Demon Deacons. Outside the conference, the Gamecocks went 0-4 to leave the overall record at 4-4-1. Georgia, Kansas State, Miami and Penn State inflicted losses on Carolina that kept their record even. In the early forties, such Gamecock legends as Lou Sossamon, Dutch Elston and John Leitner were making their presence known to the Gamecock nation. A disappointing 1-7-1 record in 1942 closed out Enright's initial five years in Columbia with 17 wins, 27 losses and 4 ties. But larger problems loomed on the horizon for South Carolina and the country with the advent of World War II. Coach Enright and most of his players were about to suit up in a different uniform to do battle with different foes with different agendas.

At the beginning of the war, Enright was assigned to a position at the Georgia Pre-Flight School in Athens as the head coach of the Skycracker football team. Athletics in general and football in particular were seen as avenues to more readily train our troops in physical combat and to entertain our men and women as they were readying themselves for eventual participation in World War II. Coaches like Enright were generally placed in charge of the physical training regimen for the troops, and as an adjunct they became the directors for the various sports programs that were conducted at each base. Lieutenant Enright began practice in Athens on August 14, 1943, in preparation for a typical Enright schedule consisting of powerful teams like Georgia Tech, Tulane, North Carolina Pre-Flight and Clemson. The Skycrackers, without the luxury of big-name players that year, won five out of six contests, with Enright registering his second win over Clemson, 32–6 in the season finale.

Future NFL great Pat Harder from Wisconsin was one of the few trainees with a big-time football resume, yet Enright and his staff that included future North Carolina head coach George Barclay put together a top-ten service team in 1943. The next season at the Pre-Flight School in Athens saw Enright become the athletic officer in charge of the base's physical training and athletics programs. He was then transferred to the Jacksonville Naval Air Station for the 1945 season and again was designated as the athletics officer. Enright was able to convince members of the Gator Bowl committee to invite the Gamecocks to Jacksonville to play the Demon Deacons in the first annual Gator Bowl game. After playing to a 13–13 tie during the regular season, Carolina lost to the Deacons by a score of 26–14 on New Year's Day 1946. As the wartime era came to a close, Coach Enright prepared for his return to Columbia in 1946 to take over the athletics department and the football program.

Coming off that improbable invitation to the inaugural Gator Bowl, Enright and the Gamecocks hit the turf running with back-to-back winning seasons in 1946 and 1947. With a somewhat more relaxed schedule, Carolina posted four Southern Conference wins in each of those years while besting rival Clemson both years as they amassed an overall 11-5-1 two-year record. An interesting mixture of war veterans and true freshmen was molded together by Enright and his staff to carve out the best two-year period since the early 1930s. Veterans like Grygo, Bryant Meeks, Dom Fusci, Ernie Lawhorne and Earl Dunham blended with young frosh like Bo Hagan, Pat Thrash and Red Wilson to spark the Gamecocks. A 26–14 Big Thursday win over Clemson propelled Carolina to two additional victories over The Citadel and Maryland to give the Gamecocks an impressive 5-1 overall record. Then two season-ending lopsided losses to Duke and Wake Forest brought USC down to earth as they finished with a 5-3 record that year. Fullback Bobby Giles and freshman halfback Bishop Strickland added some pizzazz to the offensive attack in 1947 when three placement kicks by Pete Lane proved to be the margin for another win over Clemson. That victory jump-started the Gamecocks as they finished the season with five wins and a tie to forge the best record percentage-wise in university history since the 1907 season. Early season losses to Maryland and Ole Miss were the only blemishes on the record-setting mark.

Even with the arrival in 1948 of halfback Steve Wadiak to team up with quarterback Hagan, halfback Strickland and fullback Giles, the Gamecocks' gridiron fortunes spiraled downward for the next three years. The only consolations were the record-breaking running of Wadiak and Strickland, as well as the break-even record against Clemson with one victory, one loss and one tie over the three-year span. Both Wadiak and Strickland ended up in the Gamecock record book with outstanding rushing statistics over their respective four-year careers as running backs. Finally in Wadiak's senior year (1951), Carolina reversed its three-year skid with a 5-4 mark that featured a 20–0 shutout win over Clemson, as well as an impressive 21–6 season-ending triumph over old nemesis Wake Forest. Wadiak's rushing remained

Famous Coaches of the Palmetto State

Coach Rex Enright is here with his Georgia Pre-Flight coaching staff in August 1943 prior to the first practice that year. Scheduled games that season were with Newberry, Tulane, University of Georgia, Georgia Tech and Clemson. *From left to right*: George Barclay, future head coach at W&L and UNC; Andy Pilney, future head coach at Tulane; Enright; and Bud Kerr, future head coach at Dayton. *Courtesy of John Daye, Irmo, South Carolina.*

the catalyst in Enright's offense, but a new-fangled passing attack arrived on the scene that year with quarterbacks Dick Balka and sophomore sensation Johnny Gramling. After Wadiak's graduation, the passing attack took center stage for the last four years of Coach Enright's coaching tenure. Those four years produced twenty-one wins for Enright's Gamecocks with a sterling 7-3 record in 1953 highlighting that section of the Enright era. Orangeburg County natives Gramling and Mackie Prickett parlayed their passing skills into a number of key wins in that four-year period that included three wins over Clemson. Coach Enright's final season was not what the Gamecock headman had envisioned, as a four-game losing streak sealed his fate. But Enright and the Gamecocks came alive in the finale with a 21–14 decision over Virginia in Charlottesville to close out a rather forgettable slate in 1955.

Soon after the end of the 1955 season, Coach Enright resigned his post as head football coach in order to devote full attention to the athletics directorship. Unlike most of his predecessors and successors, Enright stepped down of his own volition and quickly announced the hiring of Jim

Tatum's right-hand man at Maryland, Warren K. Giese. He continued as athletics director at the university until April 1960, when he succumbed to a combination of a stomach ailment and a heart condition. Probably no one in the history of the University of South Carolina athletics program has ever been as revered as Rex Enright, both at the beginning of his affiliation with the university and at the end.[86]

FRANK HOWARD:
CLEMSON COACHING LEGEND, 1940–69

The longest-serving head coach in the state's football history is Frank Howard, who came to the upstate school in 1931 after a stellar career at Alabama. A native of Barlow Bend, Alabama, Howard was a star guard for the Tide in his junior and senior seasons and helped the team to an undefeated record his last year that culminated in a Rose Bowl victory over Washington State, 24–0. While starting his coaching career at Clemson under head coach Jess Neely as a line coach, Howard had other coaching duties in the off-season, typical of many others of that era. He directed the track-and-field squad during the 1930s and even headed up the baseball squad for one season during World War II. These and other duties in his early tenure at Clemson prepared Howard for his assumption of head coaching duties in 1940 when Neely resigned to take over at Rice in Houston, Texas.

Despite Howard's country ways and his love of chewing tobacco, the Alabama native proved to be the Tigers' most resilient and successful coach in their history. He directed the Tigers to their first two undefeated seasons (1948 and 1950) and six ACC titles. After helping them win their first bowl game under Jess Neely, Howard continued the tradition by leading Tiger squads to six more bowl games, in which he was 3-3. He also had a winning record in the series rivalry with South Carolina during his twenty-nine-year tenure and finally succeeded in making the Clemson-Carolina matchup a home series after the final Big Thursday game in 1959.

With Howard's long success at Clemson, coupled with his country ways, he endeared himself to Clemson fans while often enraging those of his rivals, particularly at South Carolina. While he could poke fun at his rivals quite easily, he also poked fun at himself. After Carolina's coach, Warren Giese, remarked to a reporter prior to the 1958 clash with Clemson that only God and Howard knew what goes on with IPTAY funds, Howard remarked

Clemson players hoist Coach Frank Howard after a big win, possibly at the end of the last Big Thursday victory over South Carolina in Columbia, 1959. *Courtesy of Special Collections, Clemson University Libraries, Clemson, South Carolina.*

that "Giese knows about as much about IPTAY as he does about scoring or crossing our goal line." Since Carolina had been shut out in the previous two years, the Clemson head coach had some reason to back up that statement. He added that if Carolina crossed Clemson's goal line that year, Howard would tip his hat to the other coach. After the first half ended in a 6–6 tie, it appeared that Howard would not have to repeat the action in the second half. Unfortunately for him, the Gamecocks rolled up 20 more points and won the game, 26–6. After the game, Howard told reporters, "I didn't realize how sunburned my head was going to get from the hot sun during the second half."

Howard also had a lot of give and take with his players over the years. In one of the most unusual aspects of Carolina-Clemson's long rivalry, Howard had a player who captained his team one year and then the next ended up becoming the captain of Carolina. This strange turn of events grew out of World War II. Both schools had major roles to play in the war effort. Clemson served as a training center for U.S. Army infantry officers. Carolina was a center for training U.S. Navy officers. In 1942, Cary Cox had captained the Clemson team but had signed up for the navy program. After the season, the navy soon assigned him to Columbia. As the 1943 season approached, his commanding officer approached Cox and strongly suggested that he needed to play for Carolina that season. Cox tried to demur. Not willing to take no for an answer, Cox's commanding officer then ordered him to play for his new school. Orders are orders in the armed forces, so Cox had no choice.

When the Clemson game approached, Cox feared the reaction of his old coach and called him before the match to tell him his regrets. In response, Howard told him to "play his heart out." But in the crucial play of the game, Cox caught a twenty-seven-yard pass that led to the clinching score. As he was disentangling himself from the ensuing pileup, he felt a large boot to his backside. When he turned around, Cox saw Howard glaring at him and exclaiming, "Son, I told you to play your heart out, but I didn't say nothing about catching no pass."

Howard had many players with nicknames, some that did not seem too endearing. One of these was Wyndie "Dumb-Dumb" Wyndham. Part of the undefeated teams of 1948 and 1950, Wyndham was one of Howard's hardest-hitting linemen. During a practice, Howard called a play that didn't work. Howard changed it because Wyndham seemed too close. When told to change the play by "two," the tough lineman seemed not to understand. As he tried to explain, Howard chose to emphasize his point to Wyndham and growled that he was so dumb he ought not to be one but ought to be twins. The poor fellow's teammates then started calling him "Dumb-Dumb" for emphasis, and it just stuck through the rest of his career at Clemson.[87]

Willie Jeffries:
South Carolina State Coaching Legend

Born in Union, South Carolina, Jeffries attended Sims High School in the 1950s just a couple of years after the all-black school had its ninety-six-game unbeaten streak ended in 1954. Since segregation was still the law, Jeffries had few choices for college, and like most African Americans in his community, he selected South Carolina State with the assistance of his high school coach, Floyd White, a former Bulldog running back. Jeffries played football at State from 1956 to 1960, where he developed his passion for the game and took that into high school coaching upon his graduation. His first coaching job at Granard High School in Gaffney, South Carolina, established his career on the sidelines in the all-black high school league. After another high school job in the state, Jeffries eventually took over the helm of his alma mater in 1973, where his legendary status really began.

For several years, the Orangeburg college had some poor seasons on the football field, but upon his arrival this quickly changed. Taking a 1-9 team from the previous year, Jeffries turned it around in his first year, leading South Carolina State to a 7-3-1 record. In 1976, his squad won the Black National Championship, defeating Norfolk State. During his first stint at State, Jeffries led his teams to five MEAC titles as well. But Jeffries had other goals to reach besides leading his old school in six years to a 50-13-4 mark. After the 1978 season, Jeffries left South Carolina to take on the duties of head coach at Wichita State in Kansas, becoming the first African American head coach of a Division I-A program in history. After five years at Wichita State, Jeffries left to take over at Howard University in Washington, D.C., one of his alma mater's old rivals. Then, in 1989, he returned to his roots as head coach at State once more.

For the next thirteen years, Jeffries remained the school's head coach, leading South Carolina State to seven winning seasons, including five straight from 1991 to 1995. In that stretch, the Bulldogs tied their school record for wins, going 10-2 in 1994 and capturing the MEAC championship once again, the first in eleven seasons. Jeffries stayed on until he retired in 2002, welcoming his successor and one of his former players, Buddy Pough.

Along with his success in winning games, Coach Jeffries had a very good eye for talent and coached some of the school's best players of the modern era during his tenure. Perhaps his most noted player is the legendary Harry Carson of Florence, South Carolina, who anchored Jeffries's top-rated defense in the seasons from 1973 through 1975. Carson was selected to a variety of All-American teams, including the College All-American and Kodak All-American teams. He was also the first to earn two consecutive Mid-Eastern Athletic Conference Defensive Player of the Year awards. Carson then took his football talents into the NFL, where he starred for the New York Giants, helping them to one Super Bowl title during thirteen seasons. Among the many personal all-pro awards he received during his playing days, he was named to seven All-NFL teams and nine Pro Bowls. His crowning achievement came in 2006, when Carson was inducted into the Pro Football Hall of Fame in Canton, Ohio.

Another great player who came under Coach Jeffries's eye for his last year of college football was Donnie Shell. A Whitmire High School star in upstate South Carolina, Shell's small stature seemed to preclude his playing days after high school. However, in his first year at State, his coach put him at defensive back, where his speed and athletic ability made him an all-star. In his last year in Orangeburg, the first year for Coach Jeffries at the helm, Shell helped turn around the South Carolina State team, leading them to a 7-3-1 season. In his last two seasons, the Whitmire native received MEAC All-Conference team selections, and in his senior year, he was named to the Kodak All-American team. Although not drafted in the 1974 NFL draft, Shell tried out for the Pittsburgh Steelers and within no time became one of the hardest hitters and top competitors of the Iron Curtain defense that won four Super Bowls during his distinguished professional career. During his thirteen seasons, Shell was named to five all-pro teams while starting an astounding 202 games and making a record twenty-two fumble recoveries during his NFL career.

Both Carson and Shell have distinguished themselves after their playing careers. Shell continues to serve as director of player relations for the Charlotte Panthers of the NFL. Carson lives in New Jersey, where he serves as president and CEO of a sports consulting and promotion company, Harry Carson, Inc.[88]

OTHER HEAD COACHES OF NOTE

College football has been played in South Carolina for over one hundred years, and during that time there has been a wealth of outstanding head coaches across the state. John W. Heisman started it all in the early 1900s at Clemson with his four-year stint. He was extremely successful there, with nineteen wins and a winning percentage of over .800. Having just begun its intercollegiate football program two years earlier in 1913, the administration at Presbyterian College hired Walter Johnson to head up the program. Johnson ultimately coached the Blue Hose for twenty-five seasons, winning over one hundred games during his coaching tenure in Clinton. Newberry's first coach of note was Dutch MacLean, who served seventeen years for the Indians. Two Vanderbilt graduates, Josh Cody and Jess Neely, had successful runs at Clemson in the late '20s and the majority of the '30s. Cody and Clemson claimed a couple of state championships during his tenure, as well as domination over the hated Gamecocks. Neely moved on to then Southwest Conference power Rice in 1939 after his eight years with the Tigers.

One of Billy Laval's most talented players at Furman, A.P. "Dizzy" McLeod, took over the Furman program in 1932. He left eleven seasons later with fifty-six victories and a winning percentage of .600. During that time, former Carolina captain Tatum Gressette served as the head coach at The Citadel, prior to returning to Columbia to work in the athletics department. Frank Howard at Clemson, Carolina's Rex Enright and Lonnie McMillian at Presbyterian were outstanding coaches during the '40s and '50s. A young disciple of General Robert Reese Neyland came to Wofford in 1947 and turned the Terrier program around quickly. Phil Dickens, who would later coach at Wyoming and Indiana, won forty games during his six-year stay in Spartanburg. He led Wofford to a spot in Tampa's Cigar Bowl game in 1950, where they lost to college football newcomer Florida State after leading 6–0 early in the contest. While rebuilding the Wofford program, Dickens and the Terriers went undefeated during the 1948 season with four wins after beginning the year with five consecutive ties to end up with a 4-0-5 overall record. Those five ties were by the scores of 6–6, 0–0 and three straight 7–7 deadlocks. Dickens's Tennessee defensive background enabled the young coach to advance up the coaching ladder with two major college assignments following his stay at Wofford.[89]

After having spent his early years as a high school head coach in Summerville, Harvey Kirkland assumed the head coaching position at Newberry in 1952, thus embarking on a sixteen-year stint with the Indians. Those sixteen seasons represent the longest tenure ever at the Newberry school. The next season Conley Snidow began a fourteen-year stint at Wofford that produced seventy-seven wins and laid the foundation for future Terrier success. In the latter '50s, coaches Eddie Teague and Bob King took over programs at The Citadel and Furman, respectively. King, a former standout end with the Paladins, and Teague experienced solid tenures as the two old Southern Conference rivals continued to build successful programs. Both men were immensely respected throughout the state, as well as on the two campuses.[90]

For twenty-two seasons, Cally Gault roamed the sidelines at Presbyterian, winning 127 games and establishing a reputation as one of the finest coaches ever to coach in South Carolina. Prior to his coaching days with the Blue Hose, Gault spent twelve years as the head coach at North Augusta High School, where he fashioned the second-longest non-losing streak in the history of prep football in South Carolina. He had played at Presbyterian under Head Coach Lonnie McMillian, so when his alma mater beckoned, he could not pass up the opportunity. From 1963 until 1984, Gault churned out winner after winner while becoming a coaching icon. His early years at Presbyterian were spent coaching some outstanding players, such as the Eckstein brothers, particularly Dan, who became one of PC's all-time great running backs. Endearing himself quickly to the Blue Hose faithful, Gault won the Bronze Derby battle with Newberry fourteen times in his twenty-two-year career, including seven out of the first eight years that he was at Presbyterian. He retired from coaching after the 1984 season while remaining as the athletics director for several years. Always colorful in his approach to football, Gault remains to this day one of the most successful and most respected of the Palmetto State's many head coaches.[91]

During the '70s, the state of South Carolina enjoyed several of the more renowned head coaches in its history. Coaches like the Gamecocks' Paul Dietzel and Jim Carlen; Oree Banks, Willie Jeffries and Bill Davis at South Carolina State; Newberry's Fred Herren; Bobby Ross at The Citadel; as well as Wofford's Jim Brakefield and Buddy Sasser all spent part of that decade churning out winners. Dietzel came to South Carolina from West Point, and prior to his time at Army, he led LSU to a national championship in 1958. Ross left The Citadel for a stint in the NFL with Marv Levy and the Kansas City Chiefs prior to heading up the programs at Maryland and Georgia Tech. At Tech, he produced a national championship in 1991 before moving back to the NFL as the San Diego Chargers' headman. After serving as Conley Snidow's top assistant at both Emory and Henry and Wofford for a total of seventeen years, Jim Brakefield took over in Spartanburg in 1967. He turned out consistent winners there, as well as guiding the Terriers to the NAIA national championship game in 1970 before leaving for Appalachian State in 1971.[92]

Art Baker and Red Parker each guided two different Palmetto State colleges during the '70s and '80s. Baker, an ultra-successful high school coach in South Carolina, became Furman's head coach in 1973 after serving on the staffs at Clemson and Texas Tech as an assistant. He rekindled the gridiron fire in Greenville soon after there was discussion about either deemphasizing or dropping the football program entirely in the early '70s. Bringing with him a group of his former high school assistants, two of whom followed him as Furman head coaches, Baker soon rejuvenated the moribund program. His leadership laid the foundation for the many years of success attained by both Dick Sheridan and Jimmy Satterfield, who were a part of his original staff in Greenville. Baker's five years at the helm produced twenty-seven wins and two consecutive third-place finishes in the Southern Conference. He moved on to Charleston and The Citadel in 1978, succeeding Bobby Ross, who had left for the NFL. Winning thirty games in those five years again showcased the consistency that he attained as head coach. After a year on Bobby Bowden's staff at Florida State, Baker was named to lead the program at East Carolina University in Greenville, North Carolina. His freeze option offense at The Citadel and East Carolina brought him much-deserved nationwide notoriety among his coaching peers. Baker later joined the athletic administration at Carolina and has remained there in several capacities throughout his post-coaching years.

Jimmy "Red" Parker also became well known among coaches across the country in the '60s and '70s with his veer option offense. He totaled thirty-nine victories at The Citadel in seven years, including five top-three finishes in the Southern Conference. Parker's reputation as an offensive guru catapulted him to the head coaching position at Clemson in 1973. Only one winning season in his four years there plus a last-place finish in the ACC in 1976 cost Parker his job. He has remained in coaching in the Mississippi and Arkansas areas over the years with his penchant for the veer offense. Remnants of that offense abound in today's spread offenses around the country. Parker and his offensive coaches left quite a legacy with his precise reads and attention to detail. Bob Gatling, his top offensive aide, came to USC in the 1970s with the express purpose of installing the Parker veer for the Gamecocks and Coach Dietzel.

When Jim Carlen came to USC in 1975, he had just completed successful stints at both West Virginia and Texas Tech. Carlen played and coached at Georgia Tech under the legendary Bobby Dodd prior to going to Morgantown for his first head coaching job. His top aide at West Virginia was an aspiring young coach by the name of Bobby Bowden who, in fact, replaced Carlen when he left for Texas Tech in 1970. Carlen put the Gamecocks on the national map with an outstanding running game, anchored by large, aggressive offensive linemen and excellent running backs. One of those great running backs, George Rogers, captured the Heisman Trophy in 1980 after several outstanding seasons at Carolina. His running mate Johnnie Wright was almost as effective as Rogers, and along with the aforementioned offensive line, Carlen and the Gamecocks won forty-five games during his tenure at Carolina. Defensive coordinator Richard Bell produced tough, ball-hawking defenses year after year to give USC the outstanding blend of offense and defense needed for success. Another stamp of the Carlen years was the imposing national schedule that was played. Powerhouses such as Southern Cal, Michigan and Notre Dame gave the Gamecocks great national exposure and most likely catapulted Rogers toward winning the Heisman Trophy.

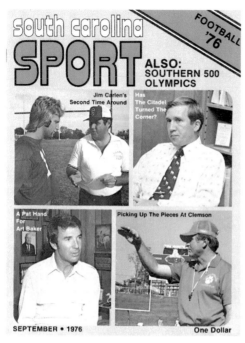

Magazine cover for *South Carolina Sport*, 1976, featuring noted coaches of that year. *Top row*: Jim Carlen (USC) and Bobby Ross (Citadel). *Bottom row*: Art Baker (Furman) and Jimmy "Red" Parker (Clemson). *Courtesy of John Daye, Irmo, South Carolina.*

Even with the success that was fashioned on the field, Carlen as athletics director and University president James Holderman were constantly at odds over finances, leading to Carlen's resignation as head coach after the 1981 season. After leaving Columbia, he took over his father's Coca-Cola business in Cookeville, Tennessee. Soon afterward, Carlen sold the business and moved to Hilton Head Island, where he remains today in private business. He has retained a home in Columbia over the years and has received many honors during that span, such as being inducted into the Texas Tech Athletic Hall of Fame, and he is in the process of being nominated for inclusion in the National Football Foundation College Football Hall of Fame in South Bend, Indiana. Carlen always takes the high road when talk of his Carolina days comes up and prefers to praise his assistant coaches and former players rather than getting caught up in the controversy surrounding his situation at USC.[93]

Dick Sheridan at Furman and SC State's Bill Davis assumed command at those schools after successful tenures as assistants. Sheridan, a former prep head coach at Orangeburg-Wilkinson and Airport High Schools, succeeded Baker in 1978 in Greenville and promptly won a Southern Conference title in his first season at the helm. Sheridan topped off his years at Furman with a Division I-AA national runner-up team in 1985. Earlier in the year, Furman defeated the NC State Wolfpack by a score of 42–20, sparking the Paladins to ten consecutive victories, including two national playoff wins. The Wolfpack athletics administration apparently liked what they saw that September day in 1985, as they enticed Sheridan to relocate to Raleigh for the 1986 season. He remained with the Wolfpack for seven years, winning fifty-two games while leading them to six bowl games during that span. Sheridan retired after the 1992 season and came back to his native state to attend to his sporting goods business on a full-time basis.[94]

Bill Davis, Willie Jeffries's top assistant at SC State from 1973 until 1978, became the head coach when Jeffries departed for Wichita State in 1979. Davis proceeded to win the Mid-Eastern Athletic Conference championship four straight years in the early 1980s. He recorded 54 victories along with a glowing .681 winning percentage in his seven years in Orangeburg. Davis coached at Savannah State, Tennessee State and Johnson C. Smith prior to his untimely death in 2001. He amassed a total of 125 wins in his twenty-one years as a head coach. At Wofford in the late '70s, a former University of North Carolina quarterback from Conway, Buddy Sasser, was elevated to the head coaching position. Sasser had served as an assistant at Wofford and Appalachian State under Brakefield prior to assuming control in Spartanburg. He amassed 36 wins over a six-year period with the Terriers before leaving for East Tennessee State in 1983. After his coaching career ended, Sasser became athletics director at Coastal Carolina on two separate occasions, as well as served as the commissioner of the Big South Conference for eight years.

Danny Ford had an auspicious beginning to his head coaching career at Clemson, following the departure of the Tigers' previous coach, Charley Pell, to the University of Florida. After nine years as an assistant coach at Alabama, Virginia Tech and Clemson, he debuted with a 17–15 win over Ohio State in the 1978 Gator Bowl. The thirty-year-old coach, youngest in Division I at the time, defeated a college football legend in a contest that truly put Clemson football on the map when he beat the legendary Woody Hayes in the latter's last game. He compiled a 96-29-4 (.760) record at Clemson, including a 6-2 bowl record. He was the third-winningest coach in the country on a percentage basis after the 1989 season. Ford also coached twenty-one All-Americans and forty-one players who went on to play in the NFL during his eleven seasons in Tigertown.

In 1981, Ford helped Clemson reach the summit of college football by winning the Division I National Championship, the first by any Clemson team. His Tigers, who were unranked in the pre-season, downed three top-ten teams during the course of the 1981 season that concluded with the victory over Nebraska in the Orange Bowl. Ford, national Coach of the Year in 1981, is still the youngest coach to win a national championship on the gridiron. He also led Clemson to a 30-2-2 record between 1981 and 1983, best in the nation. Immediately following the 1982 season, Clemson was placed on probation by the NCAA for recruiting violations. Clemson won three straight ACC titles under his guidance between 1986 and 1988. In 1989, Clemson registered a 10-2 season and top-twelve national ranking for the fourth straight season.

Ford, who always wore a block "C" cap and chewed tobacco on the sideline, closed his career at Clemson with a 27–7 win over West Virginia and its All-American quarterback Major Harris in the Gator Bowl. In the 1980s, Clemson had the nation's fifth-highest winning percentage. Ford resigned after the 1989 season amid disagreements between he and the Clemson administration over facilities improvements. He was the focal point of an NCAA investigation at that time but was completely exonerated of any wrongdoing. After taking over at Arkansas for fired head coach Jack Crowe in 1992, Joe Kines brought Ford to Fayetteville as an assistant. Ford took over for Kines in 1993, remaining at Arkansas for five years that included a SEC West championship in 1995. He retired to his Clemson farm after the 1997 season with 122 victories overall and a winning percentage of .669. Clemson football has never been the same.[95]

Ford's counterpart at Carolina during most of his Clemson years was ex–New York Giants player Joe Morrison. After Morrison retired from professional football after the 1972 season, he was named the head coach at Tennessee-Chattanooga, remaining there for seven years. His next stop was in Albuquerque at the University of New Mexico, where he stayed for three seasons prior to taking over at Carolina in 1983. Morrison's approach to football was professional in nature. During his six-year reign in Columbia, Morrison brought some of the best players in history to USC. He won thirty-nine games and posted a .580 winning percentage to top all of Carolina's modern-day coaches. Frequent bowl trips and equally exciting games against the likes of Florida State, Georgia, Pittsburgh, Nebraska, Notre Dame and arch rival Clemson gave the Gamecock faithful six years of exceedingly well-played football. A steroid scandal of national prominence black-marked the Morrison era, and as he was beginning to recover from those issues, he suffered a heart attack and passed away at the age of fifty-one. He won over one hundred games in his career and will be remembered for his "Black Magic" defenses under defensive guru Joe Lee Dunn and his all-black attire on the sideline. The notion at Williams-Brice Stadium that "if it ain't swayin', we ain't playing" is attributed to Morrison, as was the *2001: A Space Odyssey* theme music for USC team entrances for all home games. Players such as James Seawright, Del Wilkes, Harold Green, Todd Ellis, Sterling Sharpe and Robert Brooks all gained fame under the Morrison tutelage at Carolina.[96]

When Dick Sheridan left Furman for the ACC, he was replaced by his former assistant, Jimmy Satterfield, who immediately embarked on a remarkable six-year run during which he won fifty-five games along with three consecutive Southern Conference championships. Satterfield followed the 1988 national championship season with two successive conference titles en route to his glowing eight-year record at Furman. The Paladins' only losses during the championship season were to Clemson and Marshall, whom they defeated in the first round of the playoffs. By virtue of the win over Georgia Southern, Furman became the first private college to win that prestigious championship. Linebacker Jeff Blankenship and fullback Kennet Goldsmith captured post-season honors, with Blankenship becoming the Paladins' first consensus All-American, and Goldsmith winning the fabled Jacobs Blocking Trophy in the SoCon. Satterfield rounded out the post-season as he was named the state's Coach of the Year, as well as earning the Kodak and Chevrolet National Coach of the Year awards. He left Furman after the 1993 season but resurfaced at Lexington High School as the Wildcats' head mentor several years later. Remaining in Lexington for eleven years, Satterfield retired to the Greenville area in 2007.[97]

Charlie Taaffe at The Citadel and Furman's Bobby Johnson both fashioned highly successful teams during the 1990s. In his only head coaching stint, Taaffe won fifty-five games in his nine-year stay in Charleston. His Bulldogs won a Southern Conference title in 1992 and were I-AA playoff participants for three years during his stay. Mercurial quarterback Jack Douglas was the catalyst for The Citadel as he led the Bulldogs to two playoff appearances and the SoCon championship. Taaffe had a seven-year stretch in Charleston from 1988 through 1994, in which the Bulldogs won forty-nine games, the lengthiest era in The Citadel's long history with such consistent winning. Up in Greenville, Columbia native Bobby Johnson assumed the reigns at Furman in 1994 and proceeded to win sixty games in his eight years at the helm. Johnson and the Paladins started slowly but came on in a big way, winning SoCon titles in 1999 and 2001 to climax his stay at Furman. They lost to Montana University in 2001 as the Paladins played for the national championship for the third time in their history. Johnson's last three seasons produced thirty wins, the two SoCon championships and two playoff appearances for the Paladins. His extraordinary success during that three-year stretch caught the attention of Vanderbilt, which wooed Johnson to Nashville for the 2005 season.

Darryl Dickey and Tommy Spangler at Presbyterian, along with Clemson's Tommy Bowden, carved out excellent seasons during their respective tenures at the two schools. Both Dickey and Spangler averaged seven wins per year during their time in Clinton. The Blue Hose flourished offensively during the Dickey regime, and then with Spangler at the helm, they became known for their aggressive style of defense. The two went on to become assistants at Division I programs and will likely surface later in head coaching capacities. Clemson's Bowden spent close to ten years at Clemson, finishing with over seventy wins and eight bowl appearances in his more than nine years in Tigertown. Those numbers will be extremely difficult to exceed in this day of large conferences and their accompanying championship formats with very few teams ever in contention for the top rung in Division I football.[98]

Currently the Palmetto State is blessed from top to bottom with outstanding leaders on the gridiron. With coaches such as Steve Spurrier at Carolina, Wofford's Mike Ayers, David Bennett at Coastal Carolina, SC State's Buddy Pough, The Citadel's Kevin Higgins, Bobby Lamb at Furman, Jay Mills at Charleston Southern, Benedict's Stanley Conner and 2009 newcomers Dabo Swinney at Clemson, Harold Nichols at Presbyterian, Newberry's Todd Knight and North Greenville's Jamey Chadwell, the next decade of Palmetto State football will be exciting to look forward to at all levels of play. Spurrier's record and reputation at several coaching stops make him one of the nation's elite head coaches. Wofford has seen the stability of a long-term head coach pay off with playoff appearances and SoCon titles during the last several years of Ayers's tenure in Spartanburg. Bennett, a Cheraw native, has successfully built an immensely competitive program at Coastal, one that will, year in and year out, compete for Big South titles and I-AA playoff berths.

Another ultra-successful Palmetto State high school coach, Buddy Pough, is getting the proud SC State program back on track with last season's playoff appearance and another MEAC title for the Bulldogs. Higgins came out of the NFL and has in a short time put his mark on the other Bulldogs and has them primed for a title chase in the super-tough SoCon. Furman's Lamb, who had the top passing efficiency mark in state history, will certainly keep the Paladins in contention in the SoCon, as he has won a SoCon title and made two playoff appearances in his short stay in Greenville. The resurgence of Newberry football is due in total to the diligence and in-state recruiting that former head coach Zak Willis brought to the table. Newberry has quickly become a contender in the South Atlantic Conference (SAC), as well as a national Division II force, and should continue in that direction under Knight. The Harvard-bred Mills has also quickly brought the Buccaneers to the top of the Big South in a remarkably short time and will continue to contend for Big South championships. Conner has brought the neophyte Benedict program back to respectability in just two seasons and should contend for conference honors immediately. Attention will certainly be focused on Swinney and his first season at Clemson, and the same will be true for former PC quarterback Nichols at Presbyterian and ex–Charleston Southern aide Chadwell as he takes over for longtime Palmetto State coach Mike Taylor at North Greenville.

TABLE 1. South Carolina Collegiate Head Coaching Records

Last	First	College(s)	Yrs. coached	Yrs.	W	L	Tied	W-L %
Laval	Billy	Furman/ USC/ Newberry	1915–27, 1928–34, 1938–49	32	168	124	15	0.572
Howard	Frank	Clemson	1940–69	30	165	118	12	0.58
Ayers	Mike	Wofford	1988–2008	21	141	96	1	0.595
Gault	Cally	Presbyterian	1963–84	22	127	101	8	0.555
Jeffries	Willie	SC State	1973–78, 1989–2001	19	122	72	4	0.626
Johnson	Walter	Presbyterian	1915–17, 1919–40	25	102	99	19	0.507
Ford	Danny	Clemson	1979–89	11	96	29	4	0.76
Snidow	Conley	Wofford	1953–66	14	77	59	4	0.564
Kirkland	Harvey	Newberry	1952–67	16	72	77	11	0.484
Bowden	Tommy	Clemson	1999–2008	10	72	45	0	0.615
Taylor	Mike	Newberry/ NGU	1992–2002, 2004–8	16	70	104	0	0.402
Sheridan	Dick	Furman	1978–85	8	69	23	2	0.745
Satterfield	Jimmy	Furman	1986–93	8	66	29	3	0.689
Enright	Rex	USC	1938–55	15	64	69	7	0.482
McMillian	Lonnie	Presbyterian	1941–53	13	60	58	2	0.508
King	Bob	Furman	1958–72	15	60	88	4	0.407
Johnson	Bobby	Furman	1994–2001	8	60	36	0	0.625

Last	First	College(s)	Yrs. Coached	Yrs.	W	L	Tied	W-L %
Baker	Art	Furman/ Citadel	1973–77, 1978–82	10	57	48	4	0.541
Pough	Buddy	SC State	2002–8	7	57	24	0	0.704
McLeod	A.P. "Dizzy"	Furman	1932–42	11	56	37	7	0.595
Parker	Jimmy "Red"	Citadel/ Clemson	1966–72, 1973–76	11	56	59	2	0.487
Lamb	Bobby	Furman	2002–8	7	56	29	0	0.659
Taaffe	Charlie	Citadel	1987–95	9	55	47	1	0.539
Davis	Bill	SC State	1979–85	7	54	25	1	0.681
Herren	Fred	Newberry	1968–77	10	46	54	4	0.462
Teague	Eddie	Citadel	1957–65	9	45	44	2	0.505
Carlen	Jim	USC	1975–81	7	45	36	1	0.555
Bennett	David	Coastal Carolina	2002–8	7	45	23	0	0.662
McLean	Dutch	Newberry	1921–37	17	43	96	11	0.323
Neely	Jess	Clemson	1931–38	8	43	35	7	0.547
Banks	Oree	SC State	1965–72	8	43	26	1	0.621
Dietzel	Paul	USC	1966–74	9	42	53	1	0.443
Spangler	Tommy	Presbyterian	2001–6	6	42	24	0	0.636
Prause	Carl	Citadel	1922–29	8	41	32	4	0.558
Dickens	Phil	Wofford	1947–52	6	40	16	7	0.69
Morrison	Joe	USC	1983–88	6	39	28	2	0.58
Willis	Zak	Newberry	2003–8	6	39	25	0	0.609
Sasser	Buddy	Wofford	1977–82	6	36	26	3	0.577
Gressette	Tatum	Citadel	1932–39	8	34	41	3	0.455
Mills	Jay	Chas. Southern	2003–8	6	34	33	0	0.507
Johnson	Clayton	Newberry	1982–87	6	33	32	1	0.508
Hatfield	Ken	Clemson	1990–93	4	32	13	1	0.707
West	Tommy	Clemson	1994–98	5	31	28	0	0.525
Dawson	Oliver	SC State	1940–42, 1946–50	8	30	29	7	0.508
Cody	Josh	Clemson	1927–30	4	29	11	1	0.72

Famous Coaches of the Palmetto State

LAST	FIRST	COLLEGE(S)	YRS. COACHED	YRS.	W	L	TIED	W-L %
Poss	Elliott	Presbyterian	1985–90	6	29	38	1	0.434
Giese	Warren	USC	1956–60	5	28	21	1	0.57
Brakefield	Jim	Wofford	1967–70	4	28	16	0	0.636
Perry	John	Presbyterian	1991–96	6	28	37	0	0.431
Dickey	Daryl	Presbyterian	1997–2000	4	28	15	0	0.651
Scaffe	Tommy	Wofford	1927–33	7	24	38	5	0.396
Jones	Frank	Presbyterian	1957–61	5	24	22	3	0.52
Ross	Bobby	Citadel	1973–77	5	24	31	0	0.436
Woods	Sparky	USC	1989–93	5	24	28	3	0.464
Decker	Quinn	Citadel	1946–52	7	23	39	1	0.373
Young	Bill	Furman	1950–54	5	23	24	3	0.49
Scott	Brad	USC	1994–98	5	23	32	1	0.42
Williams	Bob	Clemson	1906, 1909, 1913–15	5	21	19	6	0.522
Amis	T.B. "Dad"	Furman	1928–31	4	21	13	4	0.605
Moore	Roy	SC State	1955–59	5	20	13	1	0.603
Heisman	John	Clemson	1900–3	4	19	3	2	0.833
Major	Rip	Wofford	1919, 1922–26	6	19	34	1	0.361
Carson	Jules	Wofford	1934–41	8	19	45	9	0.322
Powers	Don	Citadel	1996–2000	5	19	36	0	0.345
Brooks	Robert	SC State	1935–39	5	18	19	4	0.488
Bass	Marvin	USC	1961–65	5	17	29	4	0.38
O'Brien	Harry	Citadel	1916–18, 1920–21	5	14	15	4	0.485

Sorted by total wins at state schools

CHAPTER 7

Unsung Heroes of
State Football

The Linemen

In 1928, William P. Jacobs Jr. of Clinton wrote a letter to the sports editors of each of South Carolina's newspapers, as well as to several football officials across the state, concerning the establishment of an award for the interferers (blockers) in the Palmetto State. The gist of Jacobs's letter is as follows:

> *I recently submitted to the coaches of the colleges of the state the idea of the presentation of a loving cup, an individual medal to the best interference or team play man in the state each year.*
>
> *The reason for suggesting the idea was that he is the unsung hero on the team, the most valuable player on the team, by virtue of the fact that he is strictly a team play man, willing to take all the hard knocks, and do the hard work, and see his fellowmen get all of the credit, and that the emphasis of the idea of team play and interference is more than likely to cause the development of offensive football teams in South Carolina—something in need of which we have certainly been for some years. The coaches all enthusiastically endorse the idea.*
>
> *I am, therefore, securing the trophies and they will be presented at a banquet of the Rotary Club of Clinton, at some near future date, at which time we expect to have the coaches of the state and the winner of the medal present as our guests, as well as the judges who select the winner.*
>
> *Yours sincerely,*
> *William P. Jacobs*[99]

Thus was born the regionally famous Jacobs Blocking Trophy that is still presented today to the best blocker in the SEC, the ACC, the SoCon and the SAC. Mr. Jacobs later became the president of Presbyterian College and was also the first football player to receive a varsity letter at his alma mater. Early in 1913, several of the students at Presbyterian were encouraged by some who had played football in high school and at other colleges to request that the college establish intercollegiate football. Jacobs was active in circulating a petition among the student body, as well as making the request to the faculty and board of trustees. An announcement was made during commencement exercises in the spring of 1913 that Presbyterian College would, in fact, initiate intercollegiate football the following fall semester. There was one stipulation from the faculty and board: the football program could not involve the college in any financial loss.

Jacobs personally directed the entire operation that first year, buying the uniforms and employing and paying the coach, as well as overseeing all other expenses. He found the time to quarterback the first team, served as team manager and was the field captain along with acting as the assistant coach. At the end of the season, the first Block P Club was formed, called the

The Jacobs Blocking Trophy, 1928. This is the original trophy awarded for the best blocker in South Carolina each season, established by Presbyterian president William P. Jacobs Jr. Separate trophies were awarded to the best SEC and ACC blocker after those conferences were established. The trophy is displayed at Presbyterian Athletic Hall of Fame, Clinton, South Carolina. *Image by Susan Dugan, Columbia, South Carolina.*

"Wearers of the P"; the first certificate was awarded to Jacobs. He remained keenly interested in football during his latter years and saw the expansion of his blocking trophy to include the best blockers not only from the state but also the other conferences mentioned above.

In 1933, Jacobs duplicated the cup and began a "best blocker" presentation annually in the huge Southern Conference. Again in 1933, when the Southeastern Conference (SEC) split from the Southern Conference, he had a duplicate made to present to the best blocker in the SEC. After Dr. Jacobs's death, the Atlantic Coast Conference (ACC) formed from the Southern Conference. His sons, William and Hugh, added a fourth cup for the ACC and carried on the presentations. An award for the South Atlantic Conference (SAC) was added in 1990, and the newest will be presented in 2009 to a player from the Big South Conference.

Family members now involved in financing and continuing the awards are Jacobs's son William of Clinton and his grandchildren, William Jacobs of Greenwood; Hugh Jacobs of Columbia; Edna Jacobs Banes of Richmond, Virginia; Susan Jacobs Chesser of Aiken; and Brett Banes, great-grandson, of Nashville, Tenessee.

A plaque is given each year to the player who is voted the best blocker in each conference. Listed below are the winners of the state award since its inception in 1928, as well as some conference winners.

Table 2. Jacobs Blocking Trophy Winners

1928	O.D. Padgett	Clemson	1940	Gates Barker	Furman
1929	Hugh Stoddard	Carolina	1941	Arthur Elston	USC
1930	Grady Salley	Clemson	1942	Marion Craig	Clemson
1931	Fred Hambright	Carolina	1943	William V. McMillan	USC
1932	Bill Hutt	Furman	1944	Alton Cumbie	Clemson
1933	Bob Griffin	Furman	1945	Alton Cumbie	Clemson
1934	Harry Bolick	Presbyterian	1946	Bryan Meeks	USC
1935	Jack Shivers	Furman	1948	Robert Martin	Clemson
1936	A.A. Sabatos	Citadel	1949	Robert Prevatte	Wofford
1937	Don J. Willis	Clemson	1950	Dick Hendley	Clemson
1938	Don J. Willis	Clemson	1951	Jim Piner	Furman
1939	P.N. "June" Moore	Presbyterian	1952	"Hootie" Johnson	USC

Unsung Heroes of State Football

1953	Bill Wohrman	USC
1954	Bill Wohrman	USC
1955	Dick Marazzo	Clemson
1956	Sam DeLuca	USC
1957	Bill Thomas	Clemson
1958	John Saunders	USC
1959	Doug Cline	Clemson
1960	Jake Bodkin	USC
1961	Jim Moss	USC
1962	Jim Moss	USC
1964	Billy Ward	Clemson
1965	Bo Rufner	Clemson
1966	Wayne Mass	Clemson
1967	Harry Olszewski	Clemson
1968	Joe Lhotski	Clemson
1969	Dave DeCamilla	USC
1970	Dave Thompson	Clemson
1971	Dennis Ford	USC
1972	Johnny Jeselnik	Presbyterian
1973	Ken Peeples	Clemson
1974	Ken Peeples	Clemson
1975	Mike McCabe	USC
1976	Steve Courson	USC
1977	Joe Bostic	Clemson
1978	Joe Bostic	Clemson
1979	Roy Walker	Presbyterian
1980	George Schechterly	USC
1981	Lee Nanney	Clemson
1982	Bob Mayberry	Clemson
1983	James Farr	Clemson
1984	Del Wilkes	USC

1985	Jeff Godbee	Newberry
1986	John Phillips	Clemson
1987	John Phillips	Clemson
1988	Carlos Avalos	Citadel
1989	Steve Duggan	Furman
1990	Stacey Long	Clemson

South Atlantic Conference

1996	Brian Estes	Presbyterian
1997	Ryan Keese	Presbyterian
2005	Marcus Brisbone	Presbyterian
2006	Heath Benedict	Newberry
2007	Heath Benedict	Newberry

Southern Conference

1978	Brette Simmons	Furman
1980	Charlie Anderson	Furman
1981	Charlie Anderson	Furman
1982	Mike Coleman	Furman
1984	Dinky Williams	Furman
1985	Gene Reeder	Furman
1988	Kennet Goldsmith	Furman
1990	Steve Duggan	Furman
1999	Ben Hall	Furman
2000	Josh Moore	Furman
2001	Donnie Littlejohn	Furman
2003	Eric Deutsch	Wofford
2004	Ben Bainbridge	Furman
2008	Joel Bell	Furman

Source: Hugh Jacobs, Jacobs Blocking Trophy private files, 2008.

CHAPTER 8

Palmetto Passers

As a result of the quality of service football played during the World War II era, the landscape of offensive football changed dramatically. Offensive football was once played with a tight formation and a running game that rarely, if ever, included a flanked receiver. After the war, both the flanked receiver(s) and the quarterback became integral parts of the football scene. Prior to World War II, there were a few teams that employed a true passing attack, and those teams were generally found in the Southwest and West Coast areas of the country. But with coaches like Paul Brown, Bud Wilkinson, Jim Tatum, Don Faurot and others, the offenses became more spread out and relied on speed and quickness as never before. Although the rushing attacks were still the prevalent mode of offensive football, the passing attacks and the quarterbacks more readily became a huge factor in both college and professional football.

Even the teams that continued to employ the single- and double-wing formations as their offensive sets integrated more passing into their offenses. Those winged formations generally consisted of one or two backs positioned outside the ends and extremely close to the line of scrimmage. As in the modern-day "spread" formations, the tailback lined up approximately five to six yards deep in the backfield. The tailback almost always received the ball directly from the center, after which he would run, pass or hand the ball off, much like the "T" formation quarterbacks. When playing the "T" formation, the quarterback positioned himself directly behind the center so as to receive the ball with an underhanded motion from the center. As far as the winged formations are concerned, single wing denotes one back outside of an end on either side of the ball, and double wing denotes a back outside of both ends. In the Palmetto State, several teams retained the wing back formations while others gravitated toward the new-fangled "T" formation, which allowed for more passing opportunities.

Oddly enough, the first three passers in the Palmetto State to reach the magical 1,000-yard mark in their careers all played on single-wing teams. Bobby Gage of Clemson played four years with the Tigers while passing for 2,448 yards and twenty-four touchdowns to become the first effective passing tailback in the state. His 1948 team went undefeated at 11-0, including a victory in the 1949 Gator Bowl over Missouri, to finish eleventh in the final AP rankings. Gage was named All-Southern and All-American for the 1948 season and played two years with the Pittsburgh Steelers after graduation. The Tigers averaged twenty-five points per game using Gage and the pass very efficiently to attain their highest overall ranking in school history.

Heir apparent to Gage was Billy Hair, who passed for 1,648 yards and fourteen touchdowns in his two seasons at the helm. During both seasons, the Tigers were ranked in the top twenty at the end of the season, with the 1950 aggregate going undefeated for the second time in three years with a sterling 9-0-1 mark. Another successful bowl venture was accomplished with a 15–14 triumph over the Miami Hurricane in the 1951 Orange Bowl game. The third of the single wing tailback/passers was Wofford's Jack Beeler, who threw for 1,203 yards while leading Phil Dickens's Terriers to a 6-3-1 final record that included losses to Auburn and Florida State. Beeler was the most efficient of the early quarterbacks, as he completed 121 out of 207 for a completion ratio of .587, a mark that stood for ten years until The Citadel's Jerry Nettles commanded a 67 percent ratio.

The first "T" formation quarterback to throw for over 2,000 yards in his career was the Gamecocks' Johnny Gramling. After he shared the quarterbacking responsibilities with Dick Balka in his sophomore season and threw for 253 yards, he blossomed in 1952 with over 700 yards passing and nine touchdowns. Gramling finished his collegiate career in 1953 by leading the newly formed Atlantic Coast Conference with 1,045 yards and eight touchdowns. He also led the ACC in total offense that year while accounting for eleven touchdowns. Gramling was named the All-ACC quarterback and started at quarterback in the East-West All-Star game in San Francisco on January 2, 1954. In a losing cause that day, he completed eleven out of twenty-two passes for 114 yards and one touchdown. He spent the next two seasons at Shaw Air Force Base in Sumter, sharing the quarterback chores with Duke's Jerry Barger while on active duty. Drafted in the twenty-fourth round by the Cleveland Browns after his senior season, Gramling signed with the Canadian Football League's Ottawa Roughriders, with whom he started and played quarterback for one season. Furman's Gene Pedrick was the other quarterback who passed for over 1,000 career yards. He started for the Hurricane for two years, passing for 1,534 yards and eight touchdowns. The third Clemson tailback/passer of that era was Don King, who threw for 2,077 yards in three years (1953–55).

From 1956 through 1958, Charlie Bradshaw led Wofford to eighteen wins on the strength of his arm as he passed for 2,079 yards in those three years. Bradshaw was the state's first passer to throw for more touchdowns than interceptions, with twenty-four as opposed to fourteen picks. He led the Terriers to eighteen wins in those three seasons as Conley Snidow's quarterback. Furman's Billy Baker accumulated 2,315 career passing yards in an impressive four-year stint with the Hurricane. Baker became the first quarterback in the state to attempt four hundred passes in a career. The first Clemson Tiger quarterback of note was Harvey White, who guided the Tigers from 1957 through 1959. White passed for over 2,100 yards for eighteen touchdowns and a completion percentage just over 50 percent. He sparked the Tigers to twenty-four wins in those three years while participating in three bowl games in addition to finishing each season in the AP top twenty. After garnering All-ACC honors his senior year, he was the first player ever signed by the new American Football League entry Boston Patriots in 1960. The highest completion percentage to date was registered by The Citadel's Jerry Nettles with 177 completions out of 264 attempts for a mark of 67 percent, a record that stood the test of time from 1960 through the present era of highly efficient short passing games. Nettles led The Citadel to its only bowl win against Tennessee Tech in the December 1960 Tangerine Bowl, as well as three consecutive winning seasons for the Bulldogs.

The 1960s saw major gains for the state's passers as all of the teams had gravitated to the "T" formation or its variations, with the quarterback under center and at least one wide receiver a majority of the time. South Carolina's Dan Reeves and Mike Fair, Wofford's Warren Whittaker and Clemson's Jimmy Addison all ended their collegiate careers in the '60s with well over 2,500 total passing yards. Reeves, who went on to play running back for the Dallas Cowboys, guided Head Coach Marvin Bass's Gamecocks for three years while running and passing effectively from the quarterback position. He later became a successful head coach in the NFL with stints at Denver, New York (Giants) and Atlanta.

Palmetto Passers

Whittaker quarterbacked the Terriers for two years in the mid-'60s, leading them to two winning seasons in addition to his sterling passing accomplishments. He was one of the few early quarterbacks to throw for more touchdowns (fifteen) than interceptions (six) in his career while accumulating over 2,500 total passing yards. Addison and Fair led the Tigers and Gamecocks, respectively, from 1965 through 1967 with success, as they both passed for well over 2,000 yards in their careers. Harold Chandler (Wofford), Tony Passander (Citadel) and Sammy Hewell (Furman) were the first passers to end their careers with over 3,000 passing yards. Hewell, in fact, came within a few yards of surpassing the 4,000-yard mark in 1968 as he finished his three years in Greenville.

The most impressive numbers posted during the '60s were from Carolina's Tommy Suggs and Presbyterian's Bill Kirtland as they both exceeded the 4,000-yard barrier late in the decade. Two numbers were significant for Kirtland as he passed for over 4,000 total yards while setting a new record among quarterbacks with thirty-eight touchdown passes thrown in his career. That mark stood until the mid-'80s, again exemplifying the offensive metamorphosis that took place in the decade of the '60s relating to the way in which the game was continually changing. Suggs threw for over 4,900 yards while leading Paul Dietzel's Gamecocks from 1968 through the 1970 season. During that span, the Lamar native guided USC to its first and only ACC championship in 1969, followed by its second-ever bowl appearance against West Virginia in Atlanta's Peach Bowl. His marks for passes attempted, passes completed and total passing yards all stood in the state for the next eleven years, magnifying the impact in the '60s of the passing phenomenon that was quickly becoming the rage in college football circles.

Clemson's Tommy Kendrick ushered in the '70s with a sterling passing career that saw him accumulate close to 4,000 yards while throwing for twenty-four touchdowns from 1969 through 1971. Joining Kendrick among the elite of the early 1970s were Carter Davis (Wofford), Jeff Grantz (USC) and Harry Lynch (Citadel), as they all passed for over 3,000 yards, with Davis throwing for thirty-five touchdowns in his career in Spartanburg. Lynch, the son of Camden High School head coach Red Lynch, quarterbacked the Bulldogs under both Red Parker and Bobby Ross in his three years at the helm. Grantz was a throwback to the single-wing tailback days with his vaunted running style in addition to his prowess as a passer. His numbers were extremely gaudy for the day with his 3,440 yards passing in addition to 1,571 rushing yards for a total offensive output of 5,017 combination yards while accounting for fifty-two touchdowns in his three-year career.

Grantz led the Gamecocks to a Tangerine Bowl appearance in 1975, as well as quarterbacking the Gamecocks to their most one-sided victory over Clemson that same year. Later in the decade, Furman's David Whitehurst and David Henderson along with The Citadel's Marty Crosby all surpassed the 3,000-yard mark, while Furman's Tim Sorrells along with Carolina's Ron Bass and Garry Harper all flirted with that figure. Whitehurst went on to a career in the NFL in Green Bay and is the father of another quarterback who we will come across later.

The standard-bearer for the quarterbacks of the '70s was former Spartanburg High School sensation Steve Fuller of Clemson. Fuller surpassed the four-thousand-yard barrier while passing for twenty-two touchdowns and breaking the six-thousand-yard total offense mark in his career. He also led Clemson to two consecutive Gator Bowl appearances in the late '70s, including the infamous 17–15 victory over Ohio State in Danny Ford's initial game as Clemson's head coach. At this point in time, it can be surmised that the coaching at Furman had taken a turn for the better, especially offensively, with first Art Baker, then Dick Sheridan followed by Jimmy Satterfield and their respective protégés. As can be seen within the quarterback efficiency rating chart at the end of this section, the long line of Paladin quarterbacks has been a model of consistency in the Palmetto State.

With the advent of offensive systems such as the "run and shoot" and the spread, among others, the '80s saw a boom in passing statistics in the state. Five quarterbacks registered at least 3,000 yards passing including David Charpia of Furman, Clemson's DeShane Cameron and Mike Eppley, Chuck Fraser of Wofford and Newberry's Tim Singleton. Overcoming the once vaunted 4,000-yard mark were Furman's Bobby Lamb, Kip Allen and Robert Hill of The Citadel, Clemson's Rodney Williams and another Paladin mainstay, Frankie DeBusk, who accumulated almost 5,000 yards. At the end of the 1985 season, Newberry's Jimmy Skipper had established new standards for passes attempted, passes completed and total yards passing. His 746 attempts, 372 completions and 5,390 yards were all new marks but would stand only until the end of the decade. Skipper, a Brookland-Cayce High School product, also passed for a career total of thirty-four touchdowns while leading the Indians to twenty-five wins in his four-year starting career at Newberry. Four years later, those records would collapse under a barrage of passes thrown by Carolina's Todd Ellis, who obliterated the existing totals with 9,953 yards passing with 747 completions out of 1,350 total passes attempted. His forty-nine touchdown passes also established a new watermark for Palmetto State quarterbacks, as well as the seventy-three interceptions thrown. Ellis led the

Gamecocks to two more bowl appearances while amassing twenty-five wins in his four years at Carolina. Those statistics generally stood for the next thirteen years and are still considered the barometer by which to measure quarterbacks in South Carolina.

Two of the state's finest combination quarterbacks burst onto the scene in the early '90s. At The Citadel from 1989 through 1992, Jack Douglas was a four-year starter who accumulated modest passing statistics but along with his rushing prowess was able to set new total offensive records at The Citadel. While passing for 2,829 yards, Douglas ran for an additional 3,908 yards to amass over 6,700 yards in total offense while being responsible for sixty touchdowns scored. During the same time period at Wofford, Shawn Graves was inflicting the same punishment on the Terriers' opponents. He amassed a total of fewer than 2,000 yards passing while rushing for over 5,000 yards in his four-year career at Wofford. His total offensive output of 7,351 yards and responsibility for ninety touchdowns are still records for Terrier football.

Also in the '90s, Newberry's Tim Singleton and Hunter Spivey, Stanley Myers of The Citadel, Clemson's Brandon Streeter, SC State's Marvin Marshall and the Paladins' Philly Jones and Justin Hill all accumulated over 3,000 passing yards. Bobby Fuller, a transfer from Appalachian State, quarterbacked the Gamecocks for two seasons, amassing a total of 4,896 yards and twenty-eight touchdowns with a high quarterback efficiency rating of 132.91. Four quarterbacks surpassed 5,000 passing yards during their careers in the '90s. Furman's Braniff Bonaventure, Carolina's Anthony Wright, Newberry's Dustin Coats and Clemson's Nealon Greene all had banner careers and outstanding passing statistics. After his career at Carolina, Wright enjoyed a long career as a backup quarterback in the NFL, and Greene played professionally in the Canadian Football League for years. Topping the '90s parade of signal-callers is current Chesterfield High School head coach Steve Taneyhill, who threw for 8,872 yards in his three and a half seasons as a starter for the Gamecocks. Taneyhill passed for sixty-two touchdowns in his career, as opposed to thirty-seven interceptions, allowing him to establish a high quarterback efficiency rating. He quarterbacked South Carolina to its first bowl victory ever in 1995 with a 24–21 win over West Virginia in the Carquest Bowl.

After the turn of the century, more and more colleges have taken advantage of the proliferation of the spread offense in one form or another. Passing statistics have exploded across the board, although the numbers have remained within reason with a few exceptions. Presbyterian's Todd Cunningham, an Irmo High School graduate, became the first South

Carolinian to surpass 10,000 passing yards in his career. Coupled with a touchdown output of 111, Cunningham now sits at the top of the statistical rankings in the state.

Trailing Cunningham by a scant margin, Charleston Southern's Collin Drafts and Clemson's Charlie Whitehurst both accumulated well over 9,000 yards in passing offense during their careers. Both quarterbacks attempted over 1,300 passes and completed over 800, with Drafts finishing with the higher efficiency rating of the two at 134.41. He threw for seventy-three touchdowns as opposed to forty-four interceptions during his four-year stay at Charleston Southern. Whitehurst, son of the former Furman quarterback, finished with forty-nine touchdowns and an efficiency rating of 124.16.

Former Pelion High School quarterback Josh Stepp transferred from Furman to Newberry and established new school passing records with 7,398 yards and seventy-two touchdown passes. Current Kansas City Chiefs' starting quarterback Tyler Thigpen set the standard at Coastal Carolina with outstanding career marks of 6,598 passing yards and fifty-three touchdown passes on 486 completions from 2003 to 2006. Orangeburg-Wilkinson-bred Woodrow Dantzler raised the bar for dual-threat quarterbacks in the state with 8,798 total offensive yards in his four years at Clemson. Dantzler passed for forty-one touchdowns while rushing for twenty-seven to finish with sixty-eight for his career. With over 6,000 yards passing and over 2,000 yards rushing, Dantzler established a new mark for combination signal-callers in South Carolina. A large group of quarterbacks exceeded 5,000 passing yards in the early years of the twenty-first century. Carolina's Blake Mitchell heads the list with close to 6,000, with Furman's Ingle Martin close behind with over 5,700 yards. Next are Clemson's Cullen Harper, Phil Petty of South Carolina, The Citadel's Duran Lawson and Reese McCampbell of SC State, all with over 5,000 yards in their respective careers. Trailing the leaders were Furman's Billy Napier, SC State's Cleveland McCoy and Wofford's Travis Wilson with over 4,000 yards.

One statistic that stands out in the modern passing game is the better ratio of touchdowns to interceptions. Even with more passing attempts than ever before, the number of interceptions generally does not increase, thus allowing for more proficiency as far as the offense is concerned. Defenses in general are gearing up to thwart the longer passes by increasing the pressure on the quarterback from their front six or seven. Offensively, coaches tend to counter these defensive ploys with the short passing attack, which yields fewer interceptions and, in some cases, replaces or supplements the need for a bountiful running game.[100]

TABLE 3. South Carolina Collegiate Passing Efficiency Chart

Last	First	College	1st Yr.	Last	Total	Att.	Comp.	%	Yds.	TDs	Int.	QB PE
Lamb	Bobby	Furman	1982	1985	4	449	249	0.555	4,186	41	17	156.33
Martin	Ingle	Furman	2004	2005	2	669	410	0.613	5,751	42	22	147.64
Napier	Billy	Furman	1999	2002	4	549	356	0.648	4,756	28	20	147.16
Swilling	Hugh	Furman	1989	1992	4	214	120	0.56	1,824	16	10	143
Bonaventure	Braniff	Furman	1992	1996	4	672	412	0.613	5,379	39	17	142.64
Chandler	Harold	Wofford	1967	1970	4	371	208	0.561	3,085	22	6	142.25
Newton	Sylvelle	USC	2003	2006	4	300	170	0.567	2,474	20	13	139.27
Hill	Justin	Furman	1997	2000	4	421	232	0.551	3,607	24	15	138.76
Charpia	David	Furman	1980	1983	4	361	211	0.584	3,032	19	15	138.06
Moore	Bo	Furman	2001	2004	4	228	140	0.614	1,758	11	8	135.08
Harper	Cullen	Clemson	2005	2008	4	815	518	0.636	5,762	42	20	135.04
DeBusk	Frankie	Furman	1987	1990	4	575	304	0.529	4,984	32	27	134.65
Drafts	Collin	CSU	2003	2006	4	1,344	833	0.62	9,768	73	44	134.41
Phillips	Prince	SC State	1979	1980	2	204	80	0.392	1,918	19	15	134.22
Fuller	Bobby	USC	1990	1991	2	634	373	0.558	4,896	28	17	132.91
Thigpen	Tyler	Coastal	2003	2006	4	879	486	0.553	6,598	53	25	132.55
Dantzler	Woodrow	Clemson	1998	2001	4	796	460	0.578	6,037	41	24	132.46
Mitchell	Blake	USC	2004	2007	4	794	482	0.607	5,992	38	30	132.33
Darnell	Roscoe	SC State	1985	1986	2	220	112	0.509	1,801	16	13	131.86

Last	First	College	1st Yr.	Last	Total	Att.	Comp.	%	Yds.	TDs	Int.	QB PE
Wilson	Travis	Wofford	1998	2001	4	471	261	0.554	4,067	18	21	131.64
Taneyhill	Steve	USC	1992	1995	4	1,245	753	0.605	8,782	62	37	130.22
Bradshaw	Charlie	Wofford	1956	1958	3	276	132	0.478	2,079	24	14	129.65
McCampbell	Reese	SC State	2000	2003	4	707	384	0.543	5,230	44	26	129.64
Jones	Philly	Furman	1991	1995	4	515	306	0.594	3,721	23	16	128.63
Gray	Renaldo	Furman	2004	2007	4	438	257	0.587	3,112	21	13	128.24
Eppley	Mike	Clemson	1980	1984	4	449	252	0.561	3,354	28	26	127.87
Gage	Bobby	Clemson	1945	1948	4	278	123	0.442	2,448	24	27	127.28
Marshall	Marvin	SC State	1992	1994	3	420	187	0.445	3,257	37	25	126.83
Bryant	Sidney	CSU	2004	2007	4	180	105	0.583	1,243	11	9	126.51
Henderson	David	Furman	1976	1979	4	467	259	0.555	3,582	22	23	125.59
McCoy	Cleveland	SC State	2004	2007	4	584	310	0.531	4,168	35	24	124.59
Greene	Nealon	Clemson	1994	1997	4	805	458	0.569	5,719	35	26	124.46
Wright	Anthony	USC	1995	1998	4	796	432	0.543	5,681	38	22	124.45
Whitehurst	Charlie	Clemson	2002	2005	4	1,368	817	0.597	9,665	49	46	124.16
White	Harvey	Clemson	1957	1959	3	289	145	0.502	2,103	18	12	123.55
Fuller	Steve	Clemson	1975	1978	4	554	287	0.518	4,359	22	21	123.42
Swiggett	Darren	CSU	2002	2004	3	205	118	0.576	1,490	10	12	123
Richardson	William	Coastal	2004	2007	4	321	182	0.567	2,177	16	12	122.64

Palmetto Passers

Last	First	College	1st Yr.	Last	Total	Att.	Comp.	%	Yds.	TDs	Int.	QB PE
Grantz	Jeff	USC	1972	1975	4	455	231	0.508	3,440	26	25	122.15
Hewell	Clyde	Furman	1966	1968	3	563	313	0.556	3,993	20	21	119.43
Sills	Jake	CSU	2000	2001	2	471	261	0.554	3,099	15	22	118.85
Suggs	Tommy	USC	1968	1970	3	672	355	0.528	4,916	34	41	118.77
Ellis	Todd	USC	1986	1989	4	1,350	747	0.553	9,953	49	73	118.43
Sorrells	Tim	Furman	1977	1981	4	428	197	0.46	2,945	31	24	116.51
Cameron	DeChane	Clemson	1988	1991	4	470	257	0.547	3,300	13	15	116.4
Jordan	Homer	Clemson	1979	1982	4	479	250	0.522	3,643	15	27	115.14
Pinkins	Dondrial	USC	2000	2004	4	504	265	0.526	3,459	18	18	114.87
Streeter	Brandon	Clemson	1996	1999	4	519	294	0.566	3,504	17	26	114.15
Collier	Josh	Wofford	2004	2007	4	317	156	0.492	2,217	15	15	114.11
Whitehurst	David	Furman	1973	1976	4	468	245	0.524	3,122	22	23	114.07
Ellis	Tommy	Wofford	1959	1962	4	220	86	0.391	1,656	13	9	113.64
Simmons	Willie	Clemson	2000	2002	3	391	204	0.522	2,530	16	13	113.38
Lott	Billy	Clemson	1977	1979	3	198	105	0.53	1,385	5	7	113.05
Byrd	Eli	CSU	2005	2007	3	261	147	0.563	1,617	12	14	112.81
Petty	Phil	USC	1998	2001	4	861	454	0.527	5,652	28	29	111.87
O'Cain	Mike	Clemson	1972	1975	4	182	91	0.5	1,291	6	9	110.57
Davis	Carter	Wofford	1971	1974	4	595	271	0.455	3,838	35	27	110.07

Source: NCAA and NFL Passing Efficiency computation. Internet website, 2009.

CHAPTER 9

Rushing Leaders

Prior to the advent of statistical compilation throughout college football, there were several Palmetto State collegiate runners who were deemed to be among the best in the country. Beginning with the "Gaffney Ghost" in the early 1930s, these pre-statistical running backs carved out quite a niche for themselves, not just in the state but also on the national front. As stated before, Earl Clary spearheaded the Gamecock attack for three years, leading Billy Laval's charges to three consecutive winning seasons, as well as two victories over their Big Thursday foe, the Clemson Tigers. As with many running backs, Clary continually fought injury during his career at Carolina, but when healthy he was the best runner up to that time in the state.

Furman produced two great backs during the late '30s/early '40s era prior to World War II. First Rhoten Shetley and then Dewey Proctor experienced remarkable success as premier running backs in Greenville. Shetley was the Paladins' most valuable player in 1938, as well as being named to *Collier's* Little All-American team that year. He followed his Furman career by being drafted by the NFL Brooklyn Dodgers in 1940 as the nineteenth overall pick. Starting for two seasons as a blocking back for legendary head coach Jock Sutherland, Shetley helped the Dodgers to back-to-back winning seasons before surrendering his starting role in 1943. After the war, he played one year for the Dodgers in the old All-American Football Conference, after which he retired following the 1946 season.

Proctor succeeded Shetley as Furman's premier running threat in 1940 and immediately established himself as the next Paladin superstar. After graduation in 1942, he was drafted by the New York Giants in the third round as the twenty-first overall pick. Before he could commence with his professional career, Proctor entered the service and ended up at the Great Lakes Naval Training Center near Chicago. After two seasons with the Bluejackets, he was transferred to the Bainbridge Naval Training Station in Maryland, where he played for the star-laden Commodores. With the service football experience behind him, Proctor signed with the New York Yankees of the AAFC. He spent the next four seasons in the AAFC, first with the Yankees for two seasons and then with the Chicago Rockets for a single season before heading back to New York for his final stint with the Yankees. During his four years in the AAFC, Proctor was a fullback/ linebacker, starting for the first two seasons that he spent in New York. Both Shetley and Proctor distinguished themselves as two of South Carolina's greatest running backs in the pre– and post–World War II eras of college, service and professional football.[101]

After the war, when statistical data assumed a life of its own, Carolina's Steve Wadiak and Clemson's Fred Cone rushed to the forefront with career rushing outputs of over two thousand yards each. Both Wadiak and Cone assumed legendary status at their respective schools and have been canonized over the years because of their highly unusual treks into Palmetto State lore. The following two short biographies certainly tend to point out the unusual nature of college football recruiting during the formative years of the sport.

Fred Cone is living proof that recruiting services and all their accompanying hype aren't necessarily the only means for recruiting great players. Cone was inducted into Clemson's Football Ring of Honor in the fall of 1997, just the fourth Clemson football player in history to receive the accolade. But he came to Clemson without having played a single down of high school football. It is perhaps the most unusual story concerning an athlete's journey to Clemson. Cone was visiting his sister in Biloxi, Mississippi, far from the haunts of his hometown, an obscure place called Pineapple, Alabama. Unbeknownst to Clemson head coach Frank Howard, Cone's sister lived next door to Howard's sister, Hazel, in Biloxi. During the years when Clemson would play Tulane in New Orleans, Howard would send Hazel a pair of tickets. "One year she sent the two tickets back," Howard remembered, "and said she'd like to have four tickets because she wanted to take the next-door neighbor to the game." That was in 1946, Cone's senior year in high school. After Cone graduated, Hazel wrote Howard a letter. "Brother, I have you a good football player, but he's never played football." Howard recalled that he had told the Clemson registrar to save him forty beds in the barracks and that Howard would turn in that many names on September 1. "When Hazel wrote me about Fred Cone, I had 39 names on that list. So I just wrote 'Fred Cone' in as the 40th name. And that's how I got probably the best football player I ever had."

Cone graduated from Moore Academy in Pineapple and came to Clemson in 1947 as a freshman, but he did not play that year. It was probably best for Cone, since he had not played high school football. He needed a year to get acclimated. When Cone began to play for the varsity in '48, Clemson football took on a different look. In the second game of his career, against NC State, Cone had the first of his eight 100-yard career rushing games while leading Clemson to an important victory. He was Clemson's top rusher (635 yards and seven touchdowns) during the 1948 season, a regular season that saw Clemson compile a perfect 10-0 record and an invitation to the Gator Bowl in Jacksonville, Florida, against the Missouri Tigers. Clemson ended up winning the game 24–23. Cone rushed for 72 yards and scored twice in the first quarter, but it was his effort on a fourth-down play that made the difference in the game. Clemson held a one-point lead and faced a fourth-and-three at the Mizzou forty-five. It was either gamble for a first down or punt and give Missouri another chance to score. As Howard would say later, "We hadn't stopped them all day so I took my chances with a running play." Cone hit a stonewall at left tackle but kept digging, slid off a little more to the outside, found a little wiggling room and mustered 6 yards and a first down at the Missouri thirty-five. Clemson retained possession those few remaining minutes and ran out the clock. Years later, Howard said that it was the most memorable play of his thirty-year career.

Despite a down year in 1949, Cone gained more yards (703) rushing and scored more touchdowns (nine) than his sophomore year. But 1950 was to bring to Clemson and Cone another undefeated season. After the expected win over Presbyterian to start the season, Clemson faced pre-season number seventeen ranked Missouri on the road. Cone gained 111 yards on twenty-one attempts, one of three Tigers over the 100-yard mark that day. In 1950, Clemson scored fifty points in three games, but Cone saved his best until his last regular season game against Auburn. Rumor had it that if Clemson scored more than a certain number of points on Auburn, the Orange Bowl bid was in its pocket. The Tigers from South Carolina blasted the Alabama Tigers 41–0. Cone gained 163 yards and scored three touchdowns on the ground with one coming on a 28-yard reception. Icing on the cake this time came against Miami in the Orange Bowl. Although Sterling Smith's tackle of the Hurricane's Frank Smith in the end zone for a safety brought a 15–14 victory Clemson's way, Cone had another outstanding game. He gained 81 yards on the ground, scored once, punted four times and returned one kickoff. The Cone-led 1948–50 Tigers are the only contingent in Clemson history that has recorded two undefeated seasons in a three-year period in addition to two major bowl victories. Cone and future Pittsburgh Steeler great Ray Mathews were the only common denominators in the starting lineup on those two teams. Cone's senior season numbers totaled 845 yards rushing and fifteen touchdowns and were school records at the time. He also set career records for rushing yards (2,183) and touchdowns (thirty-one).

A seven-year hitch with the Packers was so impressive that he was inducted into their hall of fame in 1974. One year he led the NFL in field goals. He was also a member of the Dallas Cowboys in their first year of existence in 1960. Later he returned to Clemson as its chief recruiter for ten years beginning in 1961. After Cone completed his Clemson career, Howard was still stumped as to how his sister could have predicted that her neighbor's brother would be such an outstanding football player. "He just looked so athletic jumping off of that diving board," Hazel said without skipping a beat. Although it was discovered later that Wadiak did, in fact, play high school football in Chicago, his journey to Columbia as well as his four-year career at Carolina have some intriguing similarities to that of Clemson's Fred Cone. His story is another bizarre indication of just how unscientific the recruiting process was in the post–World War II era of college football.[102]

Steve Wadiak and his storied playing career overcame a really meager beginning capped off with a glorified ending, albeit one laced with tragedy. On the night of March 9, 1952, almost four months after the South Carolina–Clemson game of 1951, Wadiak died tragically in an automobile accident near Aiken, South Carolina, thus ending the career of one of college football's greatest unknown running backs. "Wadiak the Cadillac," as he was known by University of South Carolina fans and foes alike, had just capped a brilliant four-year career with 2,878 rushing yards that still ranks fourth all-time at South Carolina. He had been selected in the third round of the 1952 NFL draft by the Pittsburgh Steelers shortly before his fatal accident. "The Cadillac," or "Steamboat Steve," was a U.S. Navy veteran of World War II, born and reared in Chicago prior to being recruited to South Carolina by Rex Enright, formerly a fullback at Notre Dame under the immortal Knute Rockne and currently head coach at South Carolina. The only other school to actively recruit Wadiak was Purdue, but an ex–South Carolina and then Chicago Bears player named

Running back sensation Steve Wadiak of the South Carolina Gamecocks lunges over the Clemson goal line in the 1950 Big Thursday game. That year's rivalry game ended in a 14–14 tie. *Courtesy of John Daye, Irmo, South Carolina.*

Bill Milner convinced Enright to take the unknown Wadiak, and the rest is deeply embedded in Gamecock gridiron lore.

Beginning with his freshman year in 1948, "The Cadillac" carved his niche in football by rushing for 420 yards on 51 carries, including a rather inauspicious start in the annual Big Thursday game against Clemson. On his first carry ever against Clemson, Wadiak ran for 43 yards, but late in the game he lost a fumble deep in his own territory. Although the Gamecocks stopped Clemson after that fumble, Wadiak vowed to never lose to the hated Tigers again after that 13–7 loss in his first season. During his sophomore season in 1949, Wadiak upped his rushing total to 775 yards on 152 carries, although the Gamecocks suffered through another losing season with an overall record of 4-6. The shining moment of that season was the 27–13 victory over Clemson in which "The Cadillac" scored one touchdown and set up another with a 59-yard kickoff return.

Prior to the 1950 season, Wadiak was beginning to gain both regional and national acclaim as a running back. He set a Southern Conference record with 998 rushing yards, breaking the old mark set by the legendary

"Choo-Choo" Justice of North Carolina. Again, Wadiak had an outstanding performance on Big Thursday, carrying the ball nineteen times for 256 yards (13.5 yards per carry) while scoring both South Carolina touchdowns in a 14–14 tie game. Following the season he was named player of the year in the Southern Conference, as well as captain of the All-South team, and was a unanimous selection for the All–Southern Conference team. He was also selected as an All-American on both the Williamson and Helms Foundation teams for 1950. As a result of that great season of 1950, Wadiak was also depicted on a Topps Magic trading card that featured some of the greatest college stars of that era.

Even though his rushing yardage was down during his senior season, Wadiak and the Gamecocks finished with a winning record of 5-4 along with a convincing 20–0 victory over arch rival Clemson. "Steamboat Steve" finished the year with 685 rushing yards after playing the first four games with a broken rib suffered during a pre-season scrimmage. Although his senior season was not up to his previous years statistically, Wadiak still received several post-season honors. He was named to the *Collier's Magazine* All-South team by its All-American board of coaches. Some of the other players named were Chester native Marion Campbell of Georgia, Bob Ward of Maryland, Ray Beck of Georgia Tech, Vito Parilli of Kentucky, Hank Lauricella of Tennessee and Ed "Big Mo" Modszelewski of Maryland. The Associated Press also selected him to its prestigious All-Southern offensive team for 1951 that included such stars as Ward, Modszelewski, Bill George of Wake Forest and Billy Hair of Clemson. After his senior season, Wadiak represented South Carolina in the annual Blue-Gray all-star game followed by the Senior Bowl game in Mobile, Alabama. He scored the lone touchdown for the South seniors in an impressive performance in his final football game ever.[103]

Cone's and Wadiak's numbers stood unchallenged in the state for about a decade. Then in the '60s, Wofford running backs Ted Phelps and Clifford Boyd both eclipsed the Wadiak mark by recording over 3,000 rushing yards during their careers. Cone's existing mark of 2,172 yards at Clemson fell first to Buddy Gore and then to Ray Yauger as the bar began to steadily rise as far as rushing yardage was concerned. Don Garrick of Newberry, Wofford's Ricky Satterfield and Larry Robinson of Furman each reached the 3,000-yard career mark in the '70s. During his four-year stint at The Citadel, Stump Mitchell achieved the first 4,000-yard career mark ever in the Palmetto State. After graduating from The Citadel, Mitchell enjoyed a stellar nine-year run with the St. Louis and Phoenix Cardinals of the NFL. He achieved one 1,000-yard rushing season in 1985 and followed that with three consecutive years in which he rushed for over 700 yards. His NFL career rushing total came to 4,649 yards in nine seasons. Combined with close to 2,000 receiving yards, Mitchell wound up his career with well over 6,000 yards in total offense. Mitchell currently serves as the running backs coach for the Washington Redskins after stints with Morgan State University as head coach and nine seasons as an assistant with the Seattle Seahawks.

Bursting onto the Palmetto State gridiron scene at the same time as Mitchell was a Duluth, Georgia running back named George Rogers, whose rushing marks stand alone even after almost three decades. Rogers was highly recruited out of high school and decided to attend the University of South Carolina when Head Coach Jim Carlen told him that he could play in his freshman year. Due to his large size, he seemed destined to play fullback rather than tailback. However, the Gamecocks had two running backs who graduated at the same time, so he began his college career as the starting tailback midway through his freshman season. Rogers rushed for 1,006 yards (playing in only eight games) during his sophomore year, despite splitting time with fellow sophomore Johnnie Wright. However, it was Rogers's junior campaign that launched him into the national spotlight, as he was one of the best rushers in the country with 1,681 yards. After that season, Rogers was given second team All-American honors by the Associated Press, National Editorial Alliance, United Press International, American Football Coaches and the *Football News*.

In 1980, the stage was set when the Gamecocks returned plenty of talent that was headlined by the senior and Heisman candidate Rogers. While South Carolina's 8-3 record was good, Rogers's final season was even better. His 1,781 yards was the best in the nation and earned him a spot as a finalist for the Heisman Trophy. The Downtown Athletic Club in New York City named Rogers as the winner of the 1980 Heisman Trophy. He beat out an impressive group of players, including Pittsburgh defensive lineman Hugh Green and Georgia running back Herschel Walker. Rogers also earned spots on eight All-American teams, all first team honors. Rogers had his number "38" retired during halftime ceremonies at South Carolina's final 1980 home game. He was the first University of South Carolina player to have his jersey retired while still active at the school. Rogers left the Gamecock football program as its most successful running back, and many of his records remain after all these years. His 5,204 yards is still the highest career total by any Gamecock running back, and his thirty-one rushing touchdowns is tied with Harold Green for first. He is second on the all-time points scored list with

George Rogers, University of South Carolina Heisman Trophy winner, 1980. He gained 1,781 yards in his senior season, tops in the land. Rogers gained 100 yards or more in each of his last twenty-two collegiate games. *Courtesy of Mike Safran, Columbia, South Carolina.*

202. He also gained more than 100 yards in each of his final twenty-two college games.

While his college honors were numerous, Rogers got one of the ultimate honors in football when the New Orleans Saints made him the first pick overall in the 1981 NFL draft (one pick before the New York Giants selected Lawrence Taylor). He was the first of four Heisman Trophy winners selected by the Saints (Danny Wuerffel in 1996, Ricky Williams in 1999 and Reggie Bush in 2006 were the other three). In his first season in New Orleans, Rogers led the league in rushing with 1,647 yards, which set a high for rookies at that time. He was selected as the NFL Rookie of the Year for 1981 and earned a trip to the Pro Bowl. Rogers would spend his first four seasons in New Orleans, and his running ability is credited with bringing the Saints out of their perennial cellar. He played alongside quarterback Archie Manning in 1981 and eventually with running back Earl Campbell, who was brought in during the 1984 season. Rogers would play only three more seasons, all for the Washington Redskins. When he arrived in Washington, Hall of Fame running back John Riggins was ending his professional career, while Head Coach Joe Gibbs was trying to bring the Redskins back to glory. Rogers had some of his biggest professional successes in Washington, including another trip to the Pro Bowl and a Super Bowl title on January 31, 1988. However, he soon retired due to nagging injuries after the Redskins beat the Denver Broncos 42–10 in Super Bowl XXII. When he left the NFL, Rogers had rushed for 7,176 yards with fifty-four touchdowns in seven seasons.[104]

After the 1983 season, Furman's Stanford Jennings wound up with 3,868 career yards, thus becoming the Paladins' all-time rushing leader. Jennings, a Summerville High School graduate, spent nine seasons in the NFL, seven of which were with the Cincinnati Bengals. In Super Bowl XXIII, he scored on a memorable 93-yard kickoff return for the Bengals. Newberry's John Nesbitt, Robbie Gardner of Furman and Carolina's Harold Green all eclipsed the magic 3,000-yard mark in the '80s. Later in the 1990s, Furman's Carl Tremble and SC State's Michael Hicks surpassed the 4,000-yard barrier, while Citadel quarterback Jack Douglas, The Citadel's Everette Sands, Clemson's Raymond Priester and Vic Gilmore of Newberry all flirted with the 4,000-yard mark.

But the big news of that decade was the emergence of Wofford quarterback Shawn Graves as the primary runner in the Terrier offense. Graves, a native of Marion, ended his storied career with 5,128 rushing yards to not only lead the Palmetto State, but also set four NCAA Division II all-time records for quarterbacks—rushing yards in a single season (1,483), touchdowns by a freshman (twenty-four), touchdowns in a single season by a quarterback (twenty-four) and rushing yards per game by a quarterback (147.1). All in all, he scored seventy-two touchdowns while averaging 7.0 yards per carry as the most prolific running quarterback in Palmetto State history. The initial decade of the twenty-first century produced four running backs with over 3,000 yards (Clemson's Travis Zachery, Kevious Johnson of Wofford, SC State's DeShawn Baker and James Davis from Clemson). Furman's Louis Ivory has made the most noise so far this century with a resounding career rushing mark of 5,353 yards. Ivory accomplished his feat from 1998 through the 2001 season, thus adding his name to the burgeoning slate of Furman greats with outstanding individual statistical achievements.

Following is a list of the top running backs in the history of the state since World War II, ranked in the order of the rushing yardage gained in their careers.

Rushing Leaders

TABLE 4. Top Running Backs in the State

Last	First	College	Yrs.	No. Yrs.	Att.	Yds.	Avg.	TDs
Ivory	Louis	Furman	1998–2001	4	847	5,353	6.3	53
Rogers	George	USC	1977–80	4	954	5,204	5.5	33
Graves	Shawn	Wofford	1989–92	4	730	5,128	7.0	72
Tremble	Carl	Furman	1989–92	4	696	4,149	6.0	43
Hicks	Michael	SC State	1993–96	4	701	4,093	5.8	51
Mitchell	Stump	Citadel	1977–80	4	786	4,062	5.2	31
Priester	Raymond	Clemson	1994–97	4	805	3,966	4.9	21
Sands	Everette	Citadel	1990–93	4	741	3,926	5.3	34
Douglas	Jack	Citadel	1989–92	4	884	3,908	4.4	50
Davis	James	Clemson	2005–7	3	753	3,881	5.2	47
Jennings	Stanford	Furman	1980–83	4	650	3,868	6.0	39
Gilmore	Vic	Newberry	1997–2000	4		3,860		
Johnson	Kevious	Wofford	2003–7	4	607	3,851	6.3	32
Satterfield	Ricky	Wofford	1972–75	4	676	3,686	5.5	27
Gorrie	Steve	Presbyterian	1992–95	4		3,486		31
Porterfield	Keath	Newberry	1993–96	4		3,462		
Baker	DeShawn	SC State	2004–6	3	608	3,370	4.2	31
Phelps	Ted	Wofford	1965–68	4	712	3,282	4.6	
Nesbitt	John	Newberry	1982–85	4		3,244		

Last	First	College	Yrs.	No. Yrs.	Att.	Yds.	Avg.	TDs
Boyd	Clifford	Wofford	1968–71	4	657	3,201	4.9	30
Garrick	Don	Newberry	1969–72	4		3,131		
Gardner	Robbie	Furman	1982–86	4	537	3,102	5.8	43
Zachery	Travis	Clemson	1998–2001	4	691	3,058	4.4	41
Bennett	Brandon	USC	1991–94	4	681	3,055	4.5	28
Robinson	Larry	Furman	1973–76	4	661	3,038	4.6	25
Green	Harold	USC	1986–89	4	702	3,005	4.3	33
Flowers	Kenny	Clemson	1983–86	4	590	2,914	4.9	26
Wadiak	Steve	USC	1948–51	4	543	2,878	5.3	
Johnson	Andrew	Citadel	1973–76	4	591	2,792	4.7	
Allen	Terry	Clemson	1987–89	3	523	2,778	5.3	28
Dendy	Thomas	USC	1982–85	4	494	2,767	5.6	25
Dantzler	Woody	Clemson	1998–2001	4	591	2,761	4.7	27
McCoy	Jesse	Wofford	1999–2002	4		2,684	7.3	21
Gipson	Cedrick	Furman	2004–7	4	500	2,666	5.3	12
Felton	Jerome	Furman	2004–7	4	575	2,652	4.6	63
Broughton	Nehemiah	Citadel	2001–4	4	582	2,643	4.5	23
Wright	Johnnie	USC	1977–81	4	552	2,589	4.7	
Gore	Buddy	Clemson	1966–68	3	600	2,571	4.3	15

Rushing Leaders

Last	First	College	Yrs.	No. Yrs.	Att.	Yds.	Avg.	TDs
Wilson	Travis	Wofford	1998–2001	4	440	2,488	5.7	
Jordan	Bobby	Wofford	1968–71	4	504	2,486	4.9	35
Hodgin	Jay Lynn	USC	1972–74	3	515	2,478	4.8	23
Murphy	Maurice	Citadel	1999–2001	3	485	2,450	5.1	
Bember	Pete	Newberry	1984–86	3		2,450		
Glenn	Mike	Furman	1978–80	3	519	2,446	4.7	29
Yauger	Ray	Clemson	1968–70	3	555	2,439	4.4	16
Jones	Melvin	Wofford	1999–2002	4	549	2,410	4.4	30
Long	Kevin	USC	1973–76	4	447	2,372	5.3	
Perkins	Aundres	Coastal	2003–6	4	432	2,343	5.4	46
May	Tim	Wofford	1981–84	4	475	2,322	4.9	
McSwain	Chuck	Clemson	1979–82	4	483	2,320	4.8	23
Williams	Clarence	USC	1974–76	3	440	2,311	5.3	
Driver	Stacey	Clemson	1982–85	4	476	2,293	4.8	15
Boyd	Cory	USC	2003–7	4	464	2,267	4.9	28
Callicutt	Ken	Clemson	1973–77	3	492	2,256	4.6	11
Best	Lenny	Wofford	1978–81	4		2,237	5.8	
Muir	Warren	USC	1967–69	3	523	2,234	4.3	
Taylor	George	Newberry	1965–68	4		2,233		

LAST	FIRST	COLLEGE	YRS.	NO. YRS.	ATT.	YDS.	AVG.	TDS
Brown	Lester	Clemson	1976–79	4	505	2,228	4.5	31
Hall	Patrick	Coastal	2003–5	3	363	2,214	6.1	18
Blunt	Rodney	Clemson	1989–93	4	508	2,173	4.3	13
Cone	Fred	Clemson	1948–50	3	466	2,172	4.7	30
Flagler	Terrence	Clemson	1982–86	4	379	2,162	5.7	17
Hall	Jon	Citadel	1970–72	3	323	2,140	6.6	
Austin	Cliff	Clemson	1978–82	4	423	2,139	5.1	27
Smith	Antonio	Citadel	1995–98	4	422	2,125	5.0	
Reed	Anthony	SC State	1981–82	2	350	2,102	6.0	19
Spruill	Kenyatta	Citadel	1994–97	4	408	2,088	5.1	
Watson	Derek	USC	1999–2001	3	437	2,078	4.8	
O'Neal	Derek	SC State	1998–99	2	437	2,058	4.7	22
Myers	Stanley	Citadel	1995–98	4	606	2,055	3.4	23
Brigham	Hendley	Furman	2001–3	3	324	2,034	6.3	12
Moore	Mark	Furman	1994–97	4	365	2,025	5.5	13
Roma	Bob	Wofford	1959–62	4		2,020	6.3	
Hagood	Kent	USC	1981–85	4	365	2,014	5.5	

Sources: Charleston Southern, The Citadel, Clemson, Coastal Carolina, Furman, Newberry, North Greenville, Presbyterian, South Carolina State, University of South Carolina and Wofford Media Guides, 2008.

CHAPTER 10

Historic Rivalries

BIG THURSDAY

One of the most unique sporting events in the country expired on October 22, 1959, at the Carolina Stadium in Columbia. A crowd of over forty-six thousand witnessed the last Big Thursday football game ever played between ancient rivals Clemson and South Carolina. Longtime Clemson head coach Frank Howard had grown weary of transporting his team to Columbia every season to take on the Gamecocks. A multitude of reasons as to why the Tigers should not have to travel to the capital city every year finally won out, and the game became a more plausible "Big Saturday" affair. Crowds in excess of eighty thousand are now commonplace on the last Saturday of the season in Columbia and in Clemson. Those large crowds dwarf the size of the crowds when the series began back in 1896 at the state fairgrounds on Elmwood Avenue.[105]

This larger-than-life rivalry began rather inauspiciously as "one of the best attractions of the fair" on November 13 with wet and rainy conditions at the state fair that day. Logan Elementary School now occupies the original venue for that first Big Thursday contest. Some two thousand curious spectators were in attendance that day to watch the Gamecocks down Clemson by a score of 12–6. At the time, it was Clemson Agricultural College against the South Carolina College (CAC vs. SCC) and the Tigers versus the Jaguars. Left halfback N.W. Brooker is credited with scoring the first touchdown ever on Big Thursday with a three-yard run that gave the Gamecocks a 6–0 lead after McLaurin's next point was successful. Carolina hung on for the one-touchdown victory in the inaugural Big Thursday clash.

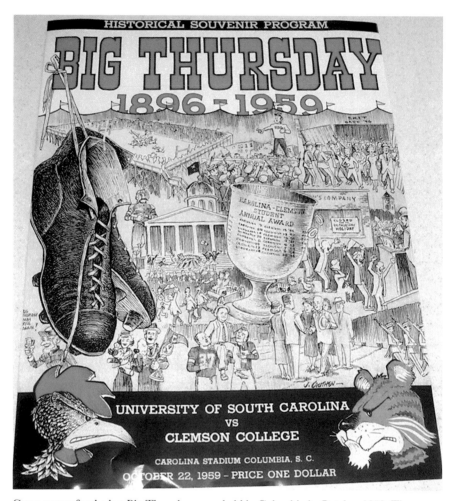

Game poster for the last Big Thursday game held in Columbia in October 1959. The following year, the Carolina-Clemson game was held at Clemson for the first time and each alternate year since then. *Courtesy of John Daye, Irmo, South Carolina.*

When John W. Heisman came to Clemson from Auburn in 1900, Tiger football fortunes immediately rose to prominence. Heisman and his Tigers demolished the Gamecocks by a score of 51–0 in the 1900 game as they scored at will in an era when scoring of any denomination was at a premium. After the 1902 game, the series was put on hold until the 1909 season, with Clemson leading the series four games to two. The two schools resumed their rivalry that year after Carolina had, in fact, dropped the sport for the 1906 season. Clemson increased its advantage in the series to five wins and two losses with another forty-nine games looming on the Big Thursday horizon.

Because of rule changes in 1912 to halt the brutality involved in college football, the sport began to take on a completely different look on the field. The dimensions of the field itself were reduced to one hundred yards with ten yards of end zone in which passes could be legally caught. Kickoffs were moved from the fifty-yard line to the forty, teams were allowed four downs to gain a first down and touchdowns became worth six points rather than five. Carolina took advantage of the rule changes that year with a convincing 22–7 triumph, with Fritz Von Kolnitz leading the way.

Although Clemson had established domination over the Gamecocks with a 13-3-1 record prior to the 1920 season, new Carolina head coach Sol Metzger achieved immediate success with two consecutive victories over the Tigers for the first time in series history. A narrow 3–0 win in 1920 followed by a convincing 21–0 triumph in 1921 temporarily alleviated the pain for the Gamecock faithful. That 1921 game drew raves nationally and spotlighted the play of center Joe Wheeler for Carolina along with future head coach John McMillan and Alex Waite. Waite scored two touchdowns that day, and McMillan intercepted a pass.

Streaks suddenly became the modus operandi in the '20s when Carolina posted three successive shutout victories from 1924 through 1926. That streak was followed by new Clemson head coach Josh Cody's four straight

That Carolina Team of 1912

This picture has significance for two reasons. One, it shows the happy 1912 Carolina squad, and some admirers, just after the Gamecocks had licked Clemson for the first time in 10 years. The other reason is that so far as known, this picture (along with some others) printed in The State the following morning was the first instance where a South Carolina newspaper printed pictures of a game the next day. The State had just put in the first photo engraving plant in South Carolina

A triumphant 1912 South Carolina Gamecock squad soon after defeating arch rival Clemson—its first victory over the Tigers in ten years. *Courtesy of the USC Archives, Columbia, South Carolina.*

wins encompassing the 1927–30 span. During that time, attendance began escalating, with crowds between ten and fifteen thousand becoming commonplace. The upward spiral in attendance mirrored a national trend with colleges across the country constructing large playing domains. Carolina quickly registered another streak with three shutout wins in succession as Coach Billy Laval's reign in Columbia was coming to an end. Clemson ended the '30s with an unprecedented seven consecutive victories as Jess Neely's stay was ending and Rex Enright's first years in Columbia were beginning with consecutive losses to Neely and the Tigers.

Frank Howard replaced Neely in 1940 and immediately developed a rivalry with Enright that lasted until Enright's retirement after the 1955 season. The 1946 game proved to be one of the best games of the series but also produced a glut of spectators never seen before or since. Bogus tickets were printed and sold, allowing thousands of people over capacity to gain admittance to the stadium. The game was played with spectators literally lining the field along the boundary lines. Carolina prevailed by a score of 26–14 in the most unusual game of the series.

Again streaks were prevalent, with Enright and the Gamecocks posting six consecutive non-losses from 1949 through 1954 with a 14–14 tie in 1950. Howard and the Tigers rebounded from that skein with three victories in a row from 1955 through 1957, followed by a huge 27–0 triumph in the series's final game in 1959. The gentlemanly Enright and the brash Howard carried on quite a contrast in style, both personally and professionally, throughout their thirteen-year terms together at the helms of the two schools. Success in the Big Thursday skirmishes afforded Enright the luxury of being held in high esteem among Gamecock supporters all over the state. Although Howard was not as successful on Big Thursdays as Enright, he achieved hall of fame status with the most wins of any gridiron head coach in the history of the state. The image of Howard blowing a kiss toward Carolina Stadium after the last game will forever live on in the hearts of Clemson Tigers everywhere.[106]

For the remainder of the twentieth century and the beginning of the twenty-first, Clemson and Carolina continued their historic rivalry on Saturdays, with venues alternating between Tigertown and Columbia. Not much has changed over that period, as the Tigers dominate the series while Carolina continues searching for another Rex Enright to keep Clemson at bay. Through the 2008 season, Clemson remained dominant, especially during the Danny Ford and Tommy Bowden tenures with the Tigers. Legendary coaches like Lou Holtz and Steve Spurrier have been hired, in part, to stem the tidal wave of victories that the Tigers have enjoyed, but to no avail. Clemson has maintained the upper hand into the twenty-first century, with hope reigning supreme for the Gamecock faithful.

TABLE 5. Big Thursday Game Results

YEAR	RESULTS	ATTENDANCE
1896	Carolina 12, Clemson 6	2,000
1897	Clemson 20, Carolina 6	2,000
1898	Clemson 24, Carolina 0	2,500
1899	Clemson 34, Carolina 0	3,000
1900	Clemson 51, Carolina 0	5,000
1902	Carolina 12, Clemson 6	3,000
1909	Clemson 6, Carolina 0	2,500
1910	Clemson 24, Carolina 0	3,500
1911	Clemson 27, Carolina 0	3,500
1912	Carolina 22, Clemson 7	3,500
1913	Clemson 32, Carolina 0	
1914	Clemson 29, Carolina 6	4,500
1915	Carolina 0, Clemson 0	
1916	Clemson 27, Carolina 0	5,000
1917	Clemson 21, Carolina 13	
1919	Clemson 19, Carolina 6	5,000
1920	Carolina 3, Clemson 0	7,000
1921	Carolina 21, Clemson 0	8,000
1922	Clemson 3, Carolina 0	8,500
1923	Clemson 7, Carolina 6	9,000
1924	Carolina 3, Clemson 0	10,000
1925	Carolina 33, Clemson 0	13,000
1926	Carolina 26, Clemson 0	12,000
1927	Clemson 20, Carolina 0	13,000
1928	Clemson 32, Carolina 0	14,000
1929	Clemson 21, Carolina 14	
1930	Clemson 20, Carolina 7	15,000

Year	Results	Attendance
1931	Carolina 21, Clemson 0	
1932	Carolina 14, Clemson 0	
1933	Carolina 7, Clemson 0	14,000
1934	Clemson 19, Carolina 0	17,000
1935	Clemson 44, Carolina 0	16,000
1936	Clemson 19, Carolina 0	18,500
1937	Clemson 34, Carolina 6	19,000
1938	Clemson 34, Carolina 12	
1939	Clemson 27, Carolina 9	18,000
1940	Clemson 21, Carolina 13	21,000
1941	Carolina 18, Clemson 14	23,000
1942	Clemson 18, Carolina 6	22,000
1943	Carolina 33, Clemson 6	16,000
1944	Clemson 20, Carolina 13	18,000
1945	Carolina 0, Clemson 0	25,000
1946	Carolina 26, Clemson 14	26,000
1947	Carolina 21, Clemson 19	
1948	Clemson 13, Carolina 7	
1949	Carolina 27, Clemson 13	35,000
1950	Carolina 14, Clemson 14	35,000
1951	Carolina 20, Clemson 0	35,000
1952	Carolina 6, Clemson 0	
1953	Carolina 14, Clemson 7	
1954	Carolina 13, Clemson 8	35,000
1955	Clemson 28, Carolina 14	35,000
1956	Clemson 7, Carolina 0	
1957	Clemson 13, Carolina 0	
1958	Carolina 26, Clemson 6	
1959	Clemson 27, Carolina 0	46,000

56 Big Thursday Games played
Clemson 32W, Carolina 22W, 2 Ties

Source: Barton, Big Thursdays and Super Saturdays.

State Championships, 1915–40

In September 1924, the FOCUS Club of Columbia established a state championship football cup to be awarded annually to the top collegiate eleven in the state. Until that announcement, there had been no definitive recognition for the best football team in South Carolina. Every college that participated in intercollegiate football was represented at that historic meeting, including all of the head coaches except two: Walter Johnson from Presbyterian, Newberry's F.D. MacLean, Billy Laval of Furman, Erskine's Robert Galloway, Bud Saunders from Clemson and South Carolina's Sol Metzger all attended the meeting. The Citadel was represented by assistant coach George Rogers, and "Plug" Osborne, former FOCUS Club member, filled in for Wofford's head coach, Rip Major.

Governor Thomas G. McLeod and the mayor of Columbia were both called upon to speak before the more than two hundred members and guests who were present at the meeting. Dr. Ralph K. Foster, who twenty years before was a standout end for South Carolina, was the presiding officer and introduced the speakers that night. Christie Benet, former United States senator and, in his day, a great tackle at Virginia, spoke on "Football as a Character Builder." Benet was also the head football coach at the University of South Carolina in the early part of the century. Former president of the SIAA (Southern Intercollegiate Athletic Association) and member of the all-time All-Southern eleven Dr. Henry D. Phillips of Sewanee spoke to the group on "The Pull of Football." It was the unanimous opinion of the members and coaches present that the endeavor to crown the champion would prove most beneficial in uniting the colleges of the state by creating a closer feeling for their in-state opponents. The coaches, players, alumni and students would gain a better understanding of the opposing teams by participating in this attempt to recognize the very best in the Palmetto State.

Late in November of the same year, the FOCUS Club's executive committee announced the personnel for the committee that would make the final decision on the winner of its state championship cup. State Senator Roach Stewart of Lancaster would serve as chairman. Stewart was captain of the 1904 and 1905 University of North Carolina grid teams. Rudolph C. Siegling of Charleston and John M. Holmes of Greenville were the two remaining members of that prestigious group. Siegling, president of the *News and Courier* at the time, was the 1909 captain at Princeton. Currently general secretary of the Greenville YMCA, Holmes was captain of the Baldwin College eleven in 1902, as well as serving later as the graduate manager and head coach at Johns Hopkins. Probably the most difficult decision in all the years of awarding the cup occurred the first season.[107]

South Carolina, Furman and Newberry each lost one game in 1924, thus creating a logjam at the top. The three-man committee determined that only Carolina and Furman would be considered, as Newberry had not played Clemson or Carolina that season. In deference to Newberry, both Clemson and Carolina were offered potential playing dates by the Indians, but for one reason or another the games were not scheduled. Final records that year indicate that Carolina, Furman, Newberry, Clemson and The Citadel were the top elevens in the state. Newberry played only one of the four opponents while the others played at least three.

Finally, the committee awarded the championship to both South Carolina and Furman, with each school housing the cup for six months. Carolina finished the 1924 season with a 6-3 overall record with in-state victories over Erskine, Presbyterian, Clemson and The Citadel while bowing to Furman by a score of 10–0. Furman completed its season with a 4-5 mark, with Palmetto State wins over Newberry and South Carolina while dropping a 6–0 decision to The Citadel. Newberry registered an 8-2 slate with in-state wins over PC, Erskine, Wofford and The Citadel while bowing Furman by a score of 14–0. The Citadel ended up at 6-4 with victories over Wofford, Furman, Clemson, Erskine and Presbyterian while losing to Newberry and Carolina. Finally, Clemson was only 2-5 with one state victory over Presbyterian while losing to Carolina and The Citadel. Furman's overall schedule was arguably the most difficult, with tilts against Alabama, Georgia, Ole Miss and Georgetown. Carolina's out-of-state foes included Georgia, NC State, North Carolina and Sewanee. Newberry's out-of-state schedule was decidedly less difficult, with contests against Lenoir-Rhyne, Rollins, Stetson and the Parris Island Marines. Earlier that year, the athletic committee of the FOCUS Club determined that in order for a school to permanently gain possession of the cup, three consecutive championships would have to be won.

For the next three years, Furman laid claim for state championship laurels with victories in key games each season. The Purple Hurricane defeated South Carolina in 1925 by the unlikely score of 2–0 to win the championship cup outright. An errant snap on an end run from punt formation was recovered by Carolina, but Rogers was downed immediately by Furman captain Tilghman just behind the goal line for the game-winning safety. For the second consecutive year, the Gamecocks were downed by Laval and his Purple Hurricane without having scored a point. Furman quarterback Whitey Rawl led Furman to another championship in 1926 with a fifty-six-yard sprint against The Citadel, giving the Hurricane the only score of the game. Five days later, Rawl and Furman trounced Clemson in Greenville by a score of 30–0 to wrap up their second successive state title. Shelby Schneider and Frank Davis were the catalysts at old Manly Field as the Hurricane staked claim to another championship. Again in 1927, the key game of the season ended with a Furman victory over the Tigers in Greenville by a tally of 28–0 before a throng of twelve thousand, the largest to ever witness a game at Manly Field. Rawl gained over one hundred yards, and Blount registered eighty-eight yards rushing as the Furman running attack was too much for Clemson again. Although the state championship continued to garner a vast amount of interest beyond the next thirteen seasons, the FOCUS Cup was permanently retired by the Purple Hurricane and was never awarded again.

Goat McMillan and the Clemson Tigers ended the Furman dominance in South Carolina the next year with a decisive 27–12 victory in Greenville. Halfback McMillan and strong line play were the keys for the Tigers as they avenged two consecutive lopsided losses to the Hurricane in state championship–type games. Riggs Field in Clemson was the site of the 1929 Clemson-Furman game that was again played for the annual state championship. Fullback Bob McCarley's placement kick was the difference for the Tigers, whose defense was led by Red Fordham and Bob Jones, who also blocked the punt that led to his touchdown reception from McMillan. A crowd of over nine thousand witnessed Clemson's second successive state championship title with the win over its fierce upstate arch rival. A fifty-five-yard punt return by a seldom-used Clemson senior catapulted the Tigers to a 12–7 win over the Purple Hurricane in Greenville. Frank Sowell etched his mark in Tiger football history by rescuing Clemson from an almost certain defeat in 1930. Coach Josh Cody ended his four-year reign at Clemson with three straight state titles and an overall record of 29-11-1 (.720) that included four consecutive victories over South Carolina.

For the first time since the 1912 season, the Gamecocks of South Carolina claimed the undivided title of state champion in 1931. A resounding 27–0 triumph over the Hurricane on November 7 allowed Billy Laval's forces to win the elusive championship. Earl Clary, the "Gaffney Ghost," was the catalyst for Carolina on both sides of the ball. His running and tackling were the key elements for the Gamecocks on homecoming day in Columbia. Coach Laval and Assistant Coach Lee Hanley were credited with devising a superior game plan that featured a liberal substitution pattern and eventually earned the victory for the home team. Even though Laval had produced many state titles for Furman, this was his first for South Carolina.

Riggs Field, Clemson's first football field, which witnessed many exciting games from 1910 until Memorial Stadium replaced it in 1942. *Courtesy of Special Collections, Clemson University Library, Clemson, South Carolina.*

One year later, the Hurricane returned to familiar territory with a 7–0 win over Clemson that enabled them to claim their first championship since the 1927 season. Bill Hutt recovered a Clemson fumble at the Tigers' eight-yard line midway through the fourth period, and Bob Griffin punched it in for the only score of the afternoon. Hutt, Griffin and future basketball head coach Lyles Alley provided the manpower prior to Griffin's one-yard plunge for the hard-fought victory. Spec Adair was perfect on the placement attempt and the Hurricane triumphed. Bill Dillard and Henry Woodward led a valiant Clemson offense as they marched toward the tying score, but a late interception by Griffin successfully thwarted their efforts.

Dizzy McLeod was in his first year at the helm in Greenville, producing a spotless Palmetto State and SIAA slate, losing only to the Cadets of West Point. Another Furman triumph over Clemson in Greenville the next season gave the Hurricane a share of the title with South Carolina in 1933. Captain Bob Smith's aerials to Gene Phillips were the keys to the 6–0 Furman win before thirteen thousand Thanksgiving Day spectators. After exchanging punts in the fourth stanza, Smith found Phillips for twenty-two yards and a first down at the Furman twenty. Then Phillips, a Gaffney native, gathered in a Smith pass for fifteen yards and the only score of the day. In desperation, Clemson executed a pass and lateral, from Shores to Dillard to Gene Willimon, moving the ball to midfield. On Clemson's final play of the game, Smith intercepted and the Hurricane shared another state title.

Jess Neely, who had assumed command at Clemson in 1931, notched his first state championship in 1934 with victories over Presbyterian, South Carolina and Furman. Although the Tigers suffered through a losing season, their 7–0 season-ending win over Furman paved the way for another title. Again the next year, Furman and Clemson battled for another championship with over fifteen thousand in attendance at Manly Field in Greenville. The Tigers opened the scoring during the first quarter when tackle Samuel Black broke through to block Roy Stevens's punt into the end zone, where Tom Brown recovered for six points. Another blocked punt figured into the final outcome when Furman's Dorn and McCarron roared through to block Horton's punt. Horton alertly sprinted into the end zone to recover the ball, giving Furman the safety rather than a touchdown. Midway through the second period, Furman's June Scott returned a Horton punt to the Clemson thirty-two. Griffin and Blair moved the ball on the ground to the seven where Blair passed to Bob King in the end zone for the go-ahead score. King missed the point after, but the scoring was over for the day, and Furman eked out another championship in a tough defensive battle.

The following season again pitted the two upstate foes against each other for the third consecutive year. Riggs Field was the site for the 1936 battle, and the Tigers were favored to regain the crown that they had surrendered the year before. But two Furman tallies in the fourth period gave the Hurricane their second straight title. After the Tigers dominated the first half but were unable to register a score, King and his Furman teammates took over. Bob Jenkins and June Scott rushed for a pair of fourth-quarter touchdowns as King and Stevens helped keep Clemson out of the end zone and the Hurricane notched another state title.

Although the Tigers and Hurricane battled to a tie on Thanksgiving Day 1937, Clemson was awarded the championship as the Tigers produced the only unbeaten record in the state. The tie was bittersweet for Clemson, as it was their only Southern Conference blemish, and dashed their hopes for an outright championship in the Southern. In one of the tightest state races in years, The Citadel, Furman and Erskine all finished with one loss, allowing the Tigers to claim the crown with only a tie against them in the state. Clemson and Carolina were both beginning to curtail their in-state schedules, with the result being that a clear-cut champion was increasingly more difficult to determine. With Banks McFadden leading the way in 1938, the Tigers earned another hard-fought victory over the game Hurricane to lay claim to the championship. Clemson managed all of its points in the second quarter as McFadden ran untouched for a ten-yard score prior to

Ben Pearson's successful eighteen-yard field goal at the end of the period. Rhoten Shetley's passing and running sparked Furman as it fought back in the second half. Shetley scored on a two-yard plunge to put the Hurricane back in the game. The game ended with Furman on the Tigers' fifteen.

All-American candidate Banks McFadden ran, passed and punted Clemson to another difficult victory over the Hurricane in 1939. Furman's Rhoten Shetley opened the scoring in the second stanza with a seventeen-yard field goal, prior to McFadden's heroics. The tide turned for the Tigers in the third quarter when McFadden's sixty-five-yard quick kick placed Furman in a predicament from which it was not able to recover. Starting at the Hurricane's forty-five, backfield mates McFadden, Charlie Timmons and Shad Bryant along with end Joe Blalock took over for the Tigers. An end-around pass from Blalock to McFadden provided the go-ahead score, and after Bryant converted, Clemson led 7–3. Shortly afterward, McFadden punted to the Hurricane's one-foot line, and Furman was backed up again. Bryant then returned the ensuing punt to the Furman twenty-four and, after one play, sprinted to the eight. From there, McFadden knifed through right tackle, carrying Furman tacklers into the end zone for the game-clinching touchdown. Bryant's conversion attempt was true, and the Tigers won another title by the score of 14–3.[108]

Conference championships soon became the goal for all of the state's teams, and talk of state championships quickly became a thing of the past. Combined with the advent of World War II, the state's collegiate teams now directed their energies in other directions, with state championships and the FOCUS Cup becoming memories, although those championships were very real for the better part of three decades in South Carolina.

A quick survey of the early years of the mythical state championship competition is warranted. South Carolina won the first title back in 1912 with convincing wins over the College of Charleston, Clemson and The Citadel. Gamecock head coach Red Edgerton coached at the College of Charleston prior to assuming control in Columbia. He remained at Carolina for four seasons, winning nineteen while losing thirteen and tying three in addition to procuring the Gamecocks' first championship. Clemson, coached by former Gamecock head coach C.R. "Bob" Williams, won successive titles in 1913 and 1914. During that two-year span, Williams and the Tigers trounced Carolina twice to ensure the two championships.

Laying claim to the state title for the next two years were the Bulldogs of The Citadel. With decisive wins over Presbyterian and Newberry followed by a 3–0 squeaker over South Carolina, the Bulldogs finished atop the standing in 1915. An even more successful season followed in 1916, as the Bulldogs won all five of their in-state contests including monumental victories over both Carolina and Clemson. The only other Citadel team that defeated both the Gamecocks and Tigers was the 1926 Bulldogs. In 1916, The Citadel finished with a glowing 6-1-1 overall record as well as a 4-1 slate in the old Southern Intercollegiate Athletic Conference. The Tigers came roaring back in 1917 by disposing of all five of their Palmetto State foes (Presbyterian, Furman, South Carolina, Wofford and The Citadel). Following that season, Head Coach Jiggs Donahue and Clemson put together another championship season with shutout victories over Carolina and The Citadel as well as a 67–7 rout of Furman. In 1919, Coach Billy Laval and the Furman Hurricane began their incredible string of state championship seasons. For the next four years, the Hurricane either won or shared the title. They won it outright in 1921 with five in-state triumphs in addition to a scoreless tie with Clemson. Carolina shared the championship with the Hurricane in 1920, while Clemson claimed a share of the crown in 1919 as a result of a season-ending 7–7 tie with Furman. Those three were involved in the only three-way tie for the title in 1922. All three won five and lost one within the confines of the state, with the results creating the logjam at the top of the standings that year. Clemson rang up another championship the season prior to the advent of the FOCUS Cup. A one-point win over the Gamecocks provided the impetus for the Tigers as they claimed their seventh title and the fifth outright championship.[109]

The early history of South Carolina collegiate football is closely entwined with the mythical state championship crowns that have been a part of the gridiron culture since the early 1900s. As one can readily determine, these championships were indeed coveted by the schools across the state, and great pride was instilled in each game against an intrastate foe. With the sport in its relative infancy in the state, it was particularly important for the players, coaches and fans alike to have the goal of winning a state title. Even the schools that were never able to produce a championship season were always aware of their standing within the borders of the state. Highly competitive contests were the rule rather than the exception as programs were being constructed to establish a presence in a conference, the Southeast and nationally. A major part of that growth occurred within the state as championship-type games were played almost every year until 1940. Conferences and national championships were outgrowths of those state title games and competitions that occurred early in the state's football history, giving each season meaning prior to the advent of bowl games and national championship games.

The Battle for the Bronze Derby

Every year for sixty years, Presbyterian College and Newberry College battled for bragging rights in their annual Bronze Derby skirmish. For several years after the end of World War II, student antagonism concerning the rivalry had been on the rise, and school administrators were growing increasingly wary of the athletic relationship between the two arch rivals. A ruckus ensued at the basketball game on January 30, 1946, and the rivalry was almost abandoned on the spot. But two clear-thinking college publicists were able to salvage tradition from what could have been a disastrous end to the athletic relations between the two neighboring denominational colleges. Prior to the start of the game, several PC students unfurled a large banner and placed it on the gymnasium wall behind the Presbyterian cheering section. The banner read "Beat Hell Out of Newberry," and the battle was on.

While attention was focused on the court, some Newberry students commandeered a ladder and placed it outside the building near a window close to the banner. Entering through the window, the Newberry students ripped the banner from the wall and disappeared into the night. When the Presbyterian cheering section noticed that the banner had been confiscated, the noise level grew riotously louder as the tension grew. The Blue Hose won the hard-fought contest by a score of 51–47, and then the fun began. Of course, the PC students demanded the return of their prized banner. Tempers flared and fisticuffs followed. Then a Newberry student snatched a derby from the head of a well-dressed Presbyterian student and vanished into the dark. Two days later, the two athletics publicists became involved in the fray. Charles McDonald, then an English professor and athletics publicist at PC, wrote to Frank Kinard at Newberry suggesting that an effort be made to recover the derby and institute it as the symbol of the rivalry between the Blue Hose and the Indians. The idea of the derby serving as the laurel of triumph in future Newberry-Presbyterian athletic contests received an enthusiastic endorsement from the Newberry students. Without revealing the identity of the perpetrator, the derby was returned to Kinard, who in turn employed the W.E. Turner and Son jewelry establishment to have the derby bronzed. The actual bronzing was handled by a firm in Columbus, Ohio, and the Bronze Derby games were initiated.[110]

During the early years of the new rivalry, the derby itself was exchanged many times. Actually, the inception took place on February 28, 1947, when the two teams played the return basketball game in Clinton. The Blue Hose squeaked out a 44–42 victory when forward Vance Logan's shot was good

Action from the Bronze Derby game, 1955, in which Newberry defeated PC 20–18. Notice that in the center left quarterback Danny Brabham is keeping out of the play after handing off, owing to his broken hand that day. *Courtesy of Danny Brabham, Columbia, South Carolina.*

with only two seconds remaining. Baseball season that year brought about another exchange of the prized derby, with Newberry capturing the laurels with a 5–2 win at Newberry. Several weeks later, PC returned the favor with a 3–2 decision over the Indians in Clinton. Presbyterian retained the derby until Thanksgiving Day 1947, when the Indians upset the favored Blue Hose by a score of 6–0 to reclaim the derby for Newberry. The following season saw Presbyterian regain the rights to the derby with a convincing 20–6 triumph over the Indians. Newberry's undefeated baseball team swept the two diamond battles the next spring, thus regaining possession of the prize until another Thanksgiving Day gridiron skirmish took place. Beginning in 1956, the derby would be awarded to the victor between the school's football warriors only, and the rivalry continued to escalate each and every Thanksgiving Day. Frank Kinard and Charles McDonald should be canonized for their vision in turning a potentially caustic situation into one of the most revered college football rivalries in the country.

A Bronze Derby replica. This example is identical to the original trophy awarded each season from 1947 to 2006 to the winner of the Presbyterian College–Newberry game. When PC went into Division I-AA football in 2007, PC ended the game. This example is located in the collection of the Newberry Athletic Department. *Image by Susan Dugan, Columbia, South Carolina.*

In order to gain the proper perspective on the sixty-year series, it is necessary to divide the rivalry into sections. To begin with, the first seventeen years of the rivalry saw the Indians win six times (including the initial game), while losing nine and tying twice. That early period is sprinkled with three mini-streaks as PC won three in a row from 1950 to 1952, Newberry repeated the same streak from 1955 to 1957 and the Blue Hose won three in succession again from 1958 to 1960. Coaches Lonnie McMillian and Frank Jones combined at the outset to win seven of twelve with two ending in ties to give Presbyterian a quick lead in the series. Only Coach Billy Laval from Newberry was able to register a winning mark during the initial era, with two wins and a loss from 1947 through 1949. When Coach Cally Gault accepted the head coaching position at Presbyterian in 1963, it marked the beginning of another winning era for the Blue Hose. He was able to garner fourteen wins over the next twenty-two years against only eight losses to register another winning era for Presbyterian. Basically, Coach Gault's record in the Bronze Derby series made it almost impossible for the Indians to ever catch up in the rivalry. During the next thirteen years of competition, Newberry really held

146

its own with six wins and a tie, including three consecutive victories from 1995 through 1997. Beginning with Daryl Dickey's second season in Clinton in 1998 and continuing through Tommy Spangler's six years there, the Blue Hose reestablished their dominance with eight wins and one loss during a span that included the longest winning streak in the series. Presbyterian won six games from 1998 through 2003 as the Blue Hose solidified their overall winning status in the Bronze Derby with thirty-six wins against twenty-one losses and three ties. A complete recapitulation of the entire series game by game follows.

TABLE 6. Bronze Derby Series

Year	Result	Year	Result	Year	Result
1947	NC 6, PC 0	1970	PC 27, NC 23	1993	PC 30, NC 13
1948	PC 40, NC 7	1971	NC 34, PC 0	1994	PC 24, NC 13
1949	NC 20, PC 14	1972	PC 17, NC 0	1995	NC 9, PC 8
1950	PC 20, NC 6	1973	NC 14, PC 3	1996	NC 21, PC 10
1951	PC 27, NC 0	1974	PC 37, NC 7	1997	NC 28, PC 22
1952	PC 14, NC 12	1975	PC 14, NC 0	1998	PC 45, NC 14
1953	Tied 7–7	1976	NC 26, PC 15	1999	PC 45, NC 35
1954	PC 20, NC 18	1977	PC 3, NC 0	2000	PC 34, NC 27
1955	NC 20, PC 18	1978	PC 26, NC 0	2001	PC 31, NC 24
1956	NC 13, PC 0	1979	PC 16, NC 15	2002	PC 14, NC 10
1957	NC 13, PC 0	1980	NC 28, PC 14	2003	PC 42, NC 14
1958	PC 22, NC 0	1981	NC 26, PC 23	2004	NC 28, PC 25
1959	PC 20, NC 6	1982	PC 21, NC 7	2005	PC 38, NC 7
1960	PC 7, NC 6	1983	NC 23, PC 0	2006	PC 10, NC 0
1961	Tied 7–7	1984	NC 25, PC 16		
1962	NC 23, PC 0	1985	Tied 24–24		
1963	PC 14, NC 7	1986	PC 35, NC 20		
1964	PC 35, NC 6	1987	PC 41, NC 0		
1965	NC 6, PC 0	1988	PC 30, NC 16		
1966	PC 28, NC 7	1989	NC 29, PC 24		
1967	PC 14, NC 0	1990	NC 24, PC 7		
1968	PC 42, NC 7	1991	PC 42, NC 17		
1969	PC 23, NC 21	1992	NC 14, PC 0		

Totals:
PC 36-21-3   .625
NC 21-36-3   .375

Source: Henry, Newberry College *(excerpts).*

Next is an examination of the coaching records for the Bronze Derby game over the entire sixty-game series. A healthy competition that flourished for sixty years and is still talked about today in Palmetto grid circles will hopefully be renewed at some point in the near future.

Table 7. Bronze Derby Coaching Records

Name	College	Record	W-L %	Years
Tommy Spangler	Presbyterian	5-1-0	.833	2001–6
Daryl Dickey	Presbyterian	3-1-0	.750	1997–2000
Frank Jones	Presbyterian	3-1-1	.700	1957–61
Gary Smallen	Newberry	2-1-0	.667	1988–90
Billy Laval	Newberry	2-1-0	.667	1947–49
Lonnie McMillian	Presbyterian	4-2-1	.643	1947–53
Cally Gault	Presbyterian	14-8-0	.636	1963–84
Elliott Poss	Presbyterian	3-2-1	.583	1985–90
Reed Charpia	Newberry	2-2-0	.500	1978–81
John Perry	Presbyterian	3-3-0	.500	1991–96
Clayton Johnson	Newberry	3-3-1	.417	1982–87
Harvey Kirkland	Newberry	5-9-2	.375	1952–67
Mike Taylor	Newberry	4-7-0	.364	1992–2002
Bill Crutchfield	Presbyterian	1-2-0	.333	1954–56
Fred Herren	Newberry	3-7-0	.300	1968–77
Zak Willis	Newberry	1-3-0	.250	2003–6
Tuck McConnell	Newberry	0-2-0	.000	1950–51
Clyde Ehrhardt	Presbyterian	0-1-0	.000	1962
Brad Senter	Newberry	0-1-0	.000	1991

Source: Newberry College and Presbyterian College Football Media Guides, 2008.

New "Kids" on the Block

Beginning in the fall of 2003, the newest rivalry in the state came to fruition. The Chanticleers of Coastal Carolina University were in their first season of competition while Charleston Southern's Buccaneers had been playing as a four-year college since 1991. Both schools played what amounted to club football prior to their respective ascents into the collegiate gridiron wars. As they played out through the '90s and early 2000s, Coastal Carolina and Charleston Southern became full-fledged members of the neophyte Big South Conference, and an intense new rivalry began.

On November 22, 2003, the first game of the new series was played in Charleston. Coastal sprinted out of the blocks with five first-half touchdowns to ensure victory and a winning record in its first year as a Division I-AA football team. Even though Coastal romped to a convincing 48–14 win, the game marked the debuts of both head coaches at their schools. David Bennett moved to Coastal from Division II powerhouse Catawba a couple of years earlier in order to build the Chanticleers from the bottom up. Even though the Buccaneers had been playing collegiately since 1991, that game in 2003 marked the end of Head Coach Jay Mills's first season at the helm. Both teams were positioning themselves to compete for Big South laurels in the near future.

As early as 2004, the game took on new meaning as the Chanticleers came into the Charleston Southern game undefeated in Big South conference play. The game was played at Coastal's Brooks Field, with the Chants repeating their 2003 victory with a resounding 56–28 triumph, giving them an unblemished mark in the Big South. A strong second half propelled Coastal to the lopsided victory. So in only their second year of conference competition, Bennett and the Chanticleers finished with a 4-0 record, and that first Big South championship was a reality. Although not evident in the final score that day, Mills and the Buccaneers were steadily building a program that would compete for the championship.

Both teams approached the 2005 game with championship aspirations, as Coastal came in undefeated in conference play in addition to sporting a glowing 9-1 record overall. Emotion was to play a part in the rivalry game for the Buccaneers after former player Eddie Gadson passed away the previous summer. Coastal had control late in the game with a 24–10 lead after scoring on a fake punt with less than three minutes left to play. Registering two touchdowns in less than three minutes allowed the Buccaneers to tie the game in regulation. Their last score came with no time left on the clock, putting the game into overtime. After both teams kicked field goals in the initial overtime period, Charleston Southern posted a touchdown in the next period and then held the Chanticleers as they forged a share of the Big South title while effectively dashing Coastal's hopes for its first berth in the FCS national playoffs.

In 2006, the same scenario existed for the Chanticleers as Charleston Southern traveled to Conway for the renewal of their annual "Battle of the Beach." Coastal did not allow a repeat of the 2005 affair, as it won decisively by the score of 31–17 to finish with a sterling 9-2 mark and the cherished playoff berth. Having to traverse to Boone, North Carolina, for their first-round meeting with eventual national champion Appalachian State presented an enviable task for the upstart Chanticleers. Falling behind 31–0 at the half proved too wide a margin to overcome—Coastal fought back during the second half to gain some respectability as it succumbed to the final tally of 45–28. Bennett and the Chanticleers made their way to the FCS playoffs in the third-shortest span of any school in history, setting lofty standards for future Coastal and Buccaneer teams.

The Chanticleers and Charleston Southern renewed their burgeoning rivalry in 2007 with Coastal maintaining the upper hand with a 41–2 victory to widen its series margin to four wins as opposed to one loss. Jumping out to a comfortable 28–0 halftime advantage allowed the Chants to cruise to a convincing victory and end their season with a record of 6-5. At Brooks Stadium the next season, the Buccaneers exacted a measure of revenge with a solid 24–0 win to finish their season with a respectable 6-6 mark. Quarterback Tribble Reese tossed two third-period touchdown passes, giving Charleston Southern a 14–0 lead while spurring its defense to complete the shutout victory. A fourth-quarter field goal and a late touchdown run added to the margin of victory as the Buccaneers enjoyed their first decisive win in the series. The win over Coastal was Charleston Southern's fourth consecutive as it ended the 2008 campaign on its most positive streak ever. As the 2009 season approaches, both Coastal and the Buccaneers are gearing up to chase front-runner Liberty in pursuit of the coveted Big South football championship.[111]

Another neophyte four-year program experiencing mixed success is that of the North Greenville University Crusaders in Tigerville. Recently becoming an NCAA Division II participant, the Crusaders achieved a pinnacle of sorts with a 2006 Victory Bowl appearance. That bowl annually features two Christian colleges or universities from across the country, with North Greenville facing Malone College from Canton, Ohio, that year. The

North Greenville University Victory Bowl title team, 2006. They defeated Malone College of Canton, Ohio, 56–28. *Courtesy of North Greenville Athletic Department, Tigerville, South Carolina.*

National Christian College Athletic Association is the governing agency for the contest, which was played at North Greenville on November 18. Coming away with a lopsided 56–28 triumph topped off a sterling season for the Crusaders as they wound up with ten wins as opposed to only two losses for their finest season since becoming a four-year school. At the end of the 2008 season, longtime coach Mike Taylor retired, and the Crusaders hired Charleston Southern assistant Jamey Chadwell to guide them as they search for prominence as a Division II football-playing school.[112]

Notes

Chapter 1

1. Undated news clipping, Furman football folder (probably January 1891 based on score found in 2008 *Furman Football Media Guide*, 199), Special Collections, Furman University Library, Greenville, South Carolina.

2. John H. Moore, "Football's Ugly Decades, 1893–1913," in Steven A Reiss, ed., *The American Sporting Experience* (West Point, NY: Leisure Press, 1984), 171–72; thanks to John Moore for providing a copy of his article.

3. John S. Watterson, *College Football: History, Spectacle, Controversy* (London: Johns Hopkins University Press, 2000), 28.

4. Watterson, *College Football*, 23–24; for Godkin's remarks quoted from the *Nation*, see Moore, "Football's Ugly Decades," 168; for early laws of the game, see David M. Nelson, *The Anatomy of the Game* (Newark: University of Delaware Press, 1991), 436–37.

5. Watterson, *College Football*, 25–28; Moore, "Football's Ugly Decades," 170–71.

6. Watterson, *College Football*, 78; Moore, "Football's Ugly Decades," 169, 178–79, 180.

7. Undated news clipping, Furman football folder.

8. Carolyn B. Matalene and Katherine C. Reynolds, eds., *Carolina Voices: Two Hundred Years of Student Experiences* (Columbia: University of South Carolina Press, 2001), 97.

9. For early intramural football at Carolina, see *Garnet and Black*, USC annual, 1912; for Newberry College, see Gordon C. Henry, ed., *God Bless Newberry College: Memories of Newberry College's Yesterday and Today* (Newberry, SC: Newberry College, 2006), 170; for Wofford College, see junior class team photo, 1904, Wofford College Archives, Spartanburg, South Carolina.

10. John Heisman published resume, Clemson, 1900, Heisman folder, Special Collections, Clemson University Libraries, Clemson, South Carolina; John Heisman, *Principles of Football* (Athens: University of Georgia Press, 2000), originally published 1922; for Wofford, see *Wofford College Journal* (December 1889): 21; and for South Carolina, see *Garnet and Black*, USC annual, 1901, Cooper Library, University of South Carolina, Columbia, South Carolina.

11. Undated newspaper clipping, Furman football file; *Wofford Journal* (January 1891): 19, Wofford College Archives, Spartanburg, South Carolina.

12. For Georgia and North Carolina, see John Stegeman, *The Ghost of Herty Field* (Athens: University of Georgia Press, 1966), 2–3, 10, 27.

13. Claflin team photo, dated 1899, is in possession of John Daye, Irmo, South Carolina, but nothing further has been found to date about the team; for early South Carolina State College football records, see "A Century of Football SC State University," *2007 Bulldog Media Guide*, 52–53, 70; *South Carolina State College Athletic Reunion, April 5–8, 1990* (this pamphlet provides more details about its early football history, including conflicting information on the college's first opponent in 1907—according to this they defeated Georgia State), South Carolina State University Library Archives, Orangeburg, South Carolina. The authors thank Elaine Nichols, history curator at the South Carolina State Museum, for locating this.

14. Schedule for College of Charleston, 1903–12, compiled by John Daye, Irmo, South Carolina.

15. The schedules for both schools are based on the football websites for Furman and Wofford that have comprehensive listings of the opponents, scores and locations from the first game they played in 1889 until the 2007 season.

16. Andrew Doyle, "Foolish and Useless Sport: The Southern Evangelical Crusade Against Intercollegiate Football," *Journal of Sport History* 24 (Fall 1997): 317, 318. The authors thank Professor Doyle for bringing this article to their attention.

17. *Our Monthly* [Presbyterian College] (November 1909): 471. The authors thank Nancy Griffith, archivist, Special Collections, Presbyterian College, for sharing this information.

18. Edited versions of the letters from Wofford and Furman, as well as Presbyterian and Erskine, were solicited by Newberry College Board Chair George Cromer in 1911 when that school began contemplating the introduction of varsity football; see Henry, *God Bless Newberry College*, 169. For the *State* articles from the Northeast, see December 6 and 20, 1905. Thanks to Ann Watts, Columbia, South Carolina, for locating these two articles; *Our Monthly* (November 1909): 471.

19. For the growing importance of football on campus, see James H. Hammond's narrative on early football at Citadel and Carolina, class of 1907, in a letter dated August 4, 1961, Hammond Papers, Manuscripts Room, South Caroliniana Library, USC, Columbia, South Carolina. Thanks to Ann Watts of Columbia, South Carolina, for locating this

account. For an account of the 1902 near riot, see Matalene and Reynolds, *Carolina Voices*, 100–102.

20. Daniel Hollis, *University of South Carolina: From College to University, 1865–1956*, vol. II (Columbia: University of South Carolina Press, 1956), 229–30.

21. Account based on James H. Hammond's recollections, 1961.

22. For the beginning of Citadel football, see Hammond narrative, 1961; for the College of Charleston, see Katherine Chaddock and Carolyn Matalene, eds., *College of Charleston Voices: Campus and Community through the Centuries* (Charleston, SC: The History Press, 2006), 95–96.

23. Chaddock and Matalene, *College of Charleston Voices*, 95–96. The authors are indebted to William Pregnall, Irvington, Virginia, for sharing his memories of his father's athletic career and a copy of his unpublished manuscript about his father.

24. Chaddock and Matalene, *College of Charleston Voices*, 96.

25. James Hammond narrative, 1961.

26. Ibid.

27. *Wofford College Journal* (December 1893): 118, Wofford College Library.

28. *Wofford College Journal* (April 1893); James Hammond narrative, 1961.

29. *Bonhomie*, 1913 (Furman annual); *Furman Hornet*, 1919, Furman football files.

30. *Bonhomie*, 1913; Henry, *God Bless Newberry College*, 176; Lowry Ware, *A Place Called Due West*, n.d. Thanks to Richard Haldeman of Due West, South Carolina, for providing this information and notes; for Presbyterian College student petition and faculty agreement to allow football, see Faculty Committee Minutes (May 29, 1913), 72, Special Collections, Presbyterian College Library, Clinton, South Carolina.

Chapter 2

31. Chaddock and Matalene, *College of Charleston Voices*, 95; College of Charleston football record came from South Carolina colleges football records file (compiled by Rich Topp, Chicago, Illinois) shown at the South Carolina State Museum exhibition Mud, Sweat, and Cheers: A History of Palmetto State Football, held August 1, 2008, through February 8, 2009; on funding problems at this time, see Walter Fraser Jr., *Charleston! Charleston!* (Columbia: University of South Carolina Press, 1991), 350; note that although published sources claim all football ended at the College after 1913, it appeared that at least one more game was played after the war, against Erskine, see the *State*, October 14, 1921.

32. For an early reference to the state association, see Presbyterian College Faculty Minutes (1913), 76, and (1914), 80; for the 1920s, see *Official Furman Football Program, 1928*, Special Collections, Furman.

33. *Official Furman Football Program, 1922*, Special Collections, Furman.

34. Ibid.; New Digs: Furman Campuses and the Evoluton of the University, 1939–1973, exhibition in special collection gallery, Furman University Library, December 2008; Furman Football Program, 1924.

35. *Garnet and Black*, USC annual, 1929; during the '20s Carolina lost seven and won just three over Furman from 1919 to 1930. Clemson's record during the same period was little better at six losses, three wins and one tie, *Furman 2008 Football Media Guide*, 199; for fan attendance, see *New York Times*, October 25, 1929. The authors thank Debra Bloom, librarian, Richland County Library, Columbia, South Carolina, for locating this article.

36. *Clemson Football '89*, media guide, 226–27; 2006 USC media guide, 123–24.

37. Hollis, *University of South Carolina*, II, 319.

38. Salaries in 2007 dollars based on "The Inflation Calculator" found at http://www.westegg.com/inflation.

39. Figures based on financial records provided by Special Collections, Presbyterian College Library, Clinton, South Carolina. Thanks to Nancy Giffith for providing these figures.

40. Ibid.; for Howard's salary, thanks to Susan Hiott, Special Collections, Clemson University Libraries.

41. "Estimated Expenses and Income Football 1935," submitted by Walter Johnson, Presbyterian College football files, Special Collections, Presbyterian College Library.

42. Frank Howard, with Bob Bradley and Virgil Parker, *The Clemson Legend* (Lincoln, NE, 1990), 156–62; *Clemson Football '89*, media guide, 30–31.

43. Ibid.

44. John M. Outz, "The History of Intercollegiate Football at Presbyterian College, Clinton, S.C.," applied project in Physical Education, University of Georgia, 1975, 49–51, copy on file at Special Collections, Presbyterian College Library; D.F. Kirven, President, Walter Johnson Club, to Presbyterian College Alumnus, October 1, 1952, Presbyterian College football files, Special Collections, Presbyterian College Library.

45. Henry Lesesne, *A History of the University of South Carolina, 1940–2000* (Columbia: University of South Carolina, 2001), 65–66.

46. Don Barton, *Big Thursdays & Super Saturdays* (West Point, NY: Leisure Press, 1981), 183–84; *Clemson Football '89*, media guide, 192.

47. John C. Griffin, *Carolina vs. Clemson, Clemson vs. Carolina: A Century of Unparalleled Rivalry in College Football* (Columbia, SC: Summerhouse Press, 1998), 116.

Chapter 3

48. Scores and opponents for this period came from *Clemson Football '89*, 227–28; and 2006 *Carolina Media Guide*, 124–25; Howard, *Clemson Legend*, 132.

49. Home states of players and total roster numbers are based on lists published in *The Little Red Book of Gamecock Football* (Mullins, SC: McMillan, 1955), 32–33, and *The Gamecocks:*

Advance Information on the USC 1948 Football Team (Mullins, SC: McMillan, 1948), 22–26; "Fusci Named to the South Carolina Hall of Fame," *Spurs and Feathers* (March 20, 1991): 7, copy in possession of authors; Dom Fusci, interview with the authors, February 2008, tape in possession of F. Hamer.

50. *Clemson Football Brochure: Tips on the Tigers*, Clemson's annual football guide, 1959, 12–16, South Carolina State Museum collection, Columbia, South Carolina.

51. Eugene Moore, interview with F. Hamer, Lake City, South Carolina, August 2007, notes in possession of Hamer; "Fusci Named to the South Carolina Hall of Fame."

52. Ron Morris, "Steve Wadiak: The Heartbreak Kid," *State*, November 2, 2008.

53. Howard, *Clemson Legend*, 77; *Clemson Football '89*, 222.

54. Tom Perrin, *Atlantic Coast Conference Football: A History Through 1991* (Jefferson, NC: McFarland & Company, Inc., 1992), 55–56, 134–35.

55. Ibid., 17, 20, 53–54; Bob Boyles and Paul Guide, *Fifty Years of College Football: A Modern History of America's Most Colorful Sport* (Wilmington, DE: Sidelines Communications, Inc., 2005), 638.

56. *Furman 2008 Football Media Guide*, 104; Official Web Site of the Southern Conference, http://www.soconsports.com.

57. *Clemson Tips* (1959), 46–47; *Little Red Book*, 1962.

58. Henry, *God Bless Newberry College*, 183.

59. Outz, "History of Intercollegiate Football," 52, 55.

60. Allen University Annual 1967, 1970, microfilm copy deposited at South Caroliniana Library, USC-Columbia; Julian Shabazz, *Roar of the Tigers! An Illustrated History of Benedict College Athletics, 1907–2005* (Clinton, SC: Awesome Records, 2006), 117, 144, 158.

61. John C. Griffin, *Moments of Glory: South Carolina's Greatest Sports Heroes* (Columbia, SC: Summerhouse Press, 1998), 144–45.

62. Ibid., 196–97.

63. http://nationalchamps.net/NCAA/database/floridastate; *2008 Wofford Football Media Guide*, 121–24, found at http://athletics.wofford.edu/sports/2008.

64. Furman 2008 Football Guide, 153, 201–3.

65. Ibid., 203.

66. Perrin, *Atlantic Coast Conference Football*, 199–200; Boyles and Guide, *Fifty Years of College Football*, 340–41.

67. *2006 Carolina Media Guide*, 131–32.

68. Boyles and Guide, *Fifty Years of College Football*, 381, 388; *Sports Illustrated* (October 22, 1984), 80–82.

69. Boyles and Guide, *Fifty Years of College Football*, 580, 588.

70. *2006 Carolina Media Guide*, 120, 129, 138, 150.

71. Ibid., 52–58.

Chapter 4

72. Howard, *Clemson Legend*, 107; John D. Briley, *Career in Crisis: Paul "Bear" Bryant and the 1971 Season of Change* (Macon, GA: Mercer University Press, 2006), 33, 35–37, 295; "Clemson Football Game Program Feature: Marion Reeves," from website http://clemsontigers.cstv.com/sports/m-footbl/spec-rel. Thanks to Susan Hiott of Clemson University Libraries for providing this link; Lesesne, *History of the University*, 143–47, 150–51. Thanks to Elizabeth West, USC archivist, for locating this; for Presbyterian College's first African American players, Nancy Griffith to authors, March 4, 2009, copy in possession of F. Hamer.

Chapter 5

73. William Pregnall, "Alex Pregnall: A Biography," unpublished manuscript; *State*, November 26, 1912; *Charleston News and Courier*, October 13, 1913; *News and Courier*, July 10, 1973. Thanks to William Pregnall and Richard Pregnall for supplying these copies to the authors.
74. *Florence Morning News*, microfilm, October and November 1921.
75. *Florence Morning News* and *State*, microfilm, 1917–65.
76. Griffin, *Moments of Glory*, 33–35; Tips of the Tigers, Clemson College, 1957, 7; Lou Sahadi, *The Clemson Tigers: From 1896 to Glory* (New York: William Morrow and Co., Inc., 1983), 84–85.
77. Griffin, *Moments of Glory*, 54–56; resume for Louis C. Sossamon, sent to F. Hamer by Mr. Sossamon, November 1991; video recording of State Museum panel on USC football during World War II, November 6, 1992, copy at the South Carolina State Museum.
78. *Florence Morning News*, www.newspaperarchive.com, microfilm, November 9, 1944.
79. Raymond Schmidt, *Football's Stars of Summer* (Lanham, MD: The Scarecrow Press, Inc., 2001).

Chapter 6

80. *Clemson Football '89*, 2; John Heisman, *Principles of Football*, 267–69; Sahadi, *Clemson Tigers*, 11–14; Heisman to Walter Camp, January 1910, Heisman file, Special Collections, Clemson University Libraries.
81. *Furman 2008 Football Media Guide*, 171–72, 199.
82. Jim Hunter, *The Gamecocks: South Carolina Football History* (Huntsville, AL: The Strode Publishers, Inc., 1975), 69–89.
83. *Florence Morning News*, www.newspaperarchive.com, microfilm, 1950–57.

84. *Chicago Tribune*, University of South Carolina Cooper Library; *Florence Morning News*, www. newspaperarchive.com, and the *State*, Richland County Public Library, microfilm. 1925–37.

85. *State*, microfilm, December 1938.

86. Hunter, *The Gamecocks*, 94–138.

87. Howard, *Clemson Legend*, 10, 15, 18–23, 63–64, 114; *Clemson Football '89*, 2–3; Barton, *Big Thursdays*, 208–9.

88. Willie Jeffries, interview with authors, February 2008, notes in the possession of F. Hamer; "100 Years of S.C. State Football," from http://www.scsu.edu/news; *State*, March 3, 1996. Thanks to Brenda Boyd, librarian at the South Carolina State Library, Columbia, South Carolina, for locating the latter two sources; Griffin, *Moments of Glory*.

89. *Wofford Football 2008 Media Guide*, 114.

90. Dick Robinson and Bob New, with Bob Lang, *The Citadel; Guts and Glory: Memorable Moments in Citadel Athletics* (Lexington, KY: Great Sports Rivalries, 1995) 39–45.

91. *Presbyterian College Football 2008 Media Guide*, 95.

92. *Wofford Media Guide*, 114.

93. Coach Jim Carlen, interview with John Daye, March 2009.

94. "Dick Sheridan," Wikipedia, the free encyclopedia, http://en.wikipedia.org/wiki/Dick_Sheridan.

95. Ibid.

96. Ibid.

97. *Furman Media Guide*, 174–75.

98. *Presbyterian Media Guide*, 93.

Chapter 7

99. *State*, microfilm, September 1928.

Chapter 8

100. Charleston Southern, the Citadel, Clemson, Coastal Carolina, Furman, Newberry, North Greenville, Presbyterian, SC State, University of South Carolina and Wofford Football media guides, 2008.

Chapter 9

101. *Furman Media Guide*, 172.

102. Clemson Tigers Internet Website, http://clemsontigers.cstv.com, 2009.

103. John Daye, "Wadiak the Cadillac," *College Football Historical Society* newsletter (August 2003): 11–12.

104. "George Rogers (American football)," Wikipedia, the free encyclopedia, http://en.wikipedia.org/wiki/George_Rogers_(American_football).

Chapter 10

105. Jack Newcombe, *The Fireside Book of Football: College and Professional from the Birth of the Game to the Present* (New York: Simon and Schuster, 1964); Furman Bisher, "The Last Big Thursday," 45–47.
106. Barton, *Big Thursdays & Super Saturdays*.
107. *State*, microfilm, September 1924.
108. *Florence Morning News*, microfilm, 1920–40.
109. Robinson, *The Citadel*, 18.
110. Henry, *God Bless Newberry College*, 200.
111. *Coastal Carolina Chanticleers 2007 Football Media Guide*, 138–41.
112. North Greenville University Athletic Website, http://ngcrusaders.com, 2009.